Information Technology for Agriculture

Indian Council of Agricultural Research (ICAR)

Dr. Balasaheb Sawant Konkan Krishi Vidyapeeth (DBSKKV)

National Agricultural Higher Education Project-Institutional Development Plan (NAHEP-IDP)

NIPA® Genx Electronic Resources & Solutions P. Ltd., New Delhi-110 034

About the Athors

Dr. Chandrahauns Chavan is a Senior Professor at Jamnalal Bajaj Institute of Management Studies (JBIMS), University of Mumbai. He is Associated with the institute since 2005. In the year 2006 at the age of 38, he became the Director of the JBIMS & leading for six years for two terms between (2006-09 & 2015-18). Almost eight years he was associated with Ministry of Corporate Affairs, Institute of Company Secretaries of India, Government of India in the capacity of Joint Director and Assistant Director (Academics). He was also holding the additional Charge of Professor cum Director of Alkesh Dinesh Modi institute of Management Studies. University of Mumbai. He begins his career as Lecturer of Business Management for MBA in 1992 under university of Pune and remain in that position for four years. He is doctorate in Business Management and M. Phil, in Business Administration, He has 30 Years of experience in the field of Industry. Teaching. Research and leading management and Professional institutions of repute.

His academic contribution and leadership has been applauding by industry and academic fraternity. He received around 26 Awards, Honors & Fellowships for outstanding contributions. Some of them are International Youth Fellowship from world education leader's forum held at Germany in 2015 in presence. He has been awarded for Academic leadership for his contribution to higher education through leading, teaching and research by Higher Education Forum of India (HEF). He has been felicitated by Ministry of Industry. Government of Maharashtra for his contribution made towards Industry 2016. listed in Top 50 national personalities in India Matters (Biographic Compendium of Indian Express 2008) for contribution to Nation and iconic intervention in India's Progress. He is certified Corporate Directors from World Council of Corporate Governance, (UK) His research areas are Information Technology & Systems, Digital Business, Artificial Intelligence. Business & Technology Strategy etc. His research work is laudable; He is reviewer & Member on editorial board of various international & National journals; his 156 Research Papers has been published in (Web of Science, ADBC, Scopus, UGC Care List, Double Blind Review) with High Impact reputed International & National Journals. Good numbers of Minor and Major Business Research Projects are on his credits. He authored and edited 5 books. Successfully guided 12 Ph. D's and 5 M Phil students and more than 1000 PG projects. He has organised & curated and conducted more than 250 Seminar, Conferences. Workshops, Symposium, FDP/MDP programmes on diversified areas of management and verticals of industry and also delivered address in more than 100 Conferences, Seminars. He played pivotal role in reforming teaching, learning process and taken various innovative and strategic initiatives to prepare twenty first century management graduates and implemented various student centric education policies at Jamnalal Bajaj Institute of Management Studies, For Academic Assignment he has travelled to Germany,

France, South Africa, Netherland and Switzerland, Dubai and an across India etc.

He was the Chairman Board of studies in System Management and Academic Council member, University of Mumbai, He is Member of Research and Review Committee (RRC) of three state Universities, Mumbai, Pune and SNDT University. He is Member board of management studies, Mumbai University and Pune University. He was member to draft on line management education policy, Govt. of India, two years he was member on E- Governance initiative and implementation committee for Govt. of Maharashtra.

Two years he was Executive Board member of Association of Indian Management Schools (AIMS). He is Member on various boards like Bombay Stock Exchange, Council of Fair Business Practices of India, Employee Federation of India, Confederation of Indian Industries (CII), Institution of Director, Bombay Management Associations. Assessor of NBA, AICTE, DTE, and various many management and professional institutions and universities etc.

Bechoo Lal, PhD. became a Member (M) of IAENG: International Association of Engineers, USA with membership (108820) in 2010, a Senior Member (SM) in 2019. I am doctorate PhD in Computer Science, PhD- Information System from University of Mumbai, Master from Banaras Hindu University (BHU), PGP- Data Science from Purdue University, USA. Currently I am working as a Associate Professor in Department of Computer Science & Engineering, KLEF- KL University Vijayawada Campus Andhra Pradesh, India. My research areas are data science, big data analytics and Machine Learning.

Information Technology for Agriculture

Compiled by

Prashant S. Bodake
Dean & Director of Instruction, DBSKKV
Co-ordinator & Principal Investigator
NAHEP-IDP, DBSKKV-Dapoli, Maharashtra

Srinivasan Iyengar
Director of Jamnalal Bajaj Institute of Management Studies
Mumbai, Maharashtra

Atul G.Mohod
Co- Principal Investigator, NAHEP-IDP, DBSKKV-Dapoli, Maharashtra

Authors

C.R. Chavan
Professor & Ex-Director
J.B.I.M.S., University of Mumbai

Bechoo Lal
Associate Professor
KL University, Hyderabad

भाकृअनुप
ICAR

Indian Council of Agricultural Research (ICAR)

Dr. Balasaheb Sawant Konkan Krishi Vidyapeeth (DBSKKV)

National Agricultural Higher Education Project-Institutional Development Plan (NAHEP-IDP)

NIPA® Genx Electronic Resources & Solutions P. Ltd., New Delhi-110 034

Citation: National Agriculture Higher Education Project Institutional Development Plan, DBSKKV, Dapoli & ICAR, New Delhi

NIPA® GENX ELECTRONIC RESOURCES & SOLUTIONS P. LTD.

101,103, Vikas Surya Plaza, CU Block
L.S.C.Market, Pitam Pura, New Delhi-110 034
Ph : +91 11 27341616, 27341717, 27341718
E-mail: newindiapublishingagency@gmail.com
Website: www.nipabooks.com

For customer assistance, please contact
Phone: + 91-11-27 34 17 17
Fax: + 91-11-27 34 16 16

ISBN: 978-93-58871-13-5

Composed and Designed by NIPA®.

भारतीय कृषि अनुसंधान परिषद
कृषि अनुसंधान भवन–II, नई दिल्ली–110012
INDIAN COUNCIL OF AGRICULTURAL RESEARCH
KRISHI ANUSANDHAN BHAVAN-II, PUSA, NEW DELHI-110012
Phone: +91-11-25841760
Email: ddg.edu@icar.gov.in, ddgedn@gmail.com, nd.nahep@icar.gov.in

Dr. Rakesh Chandra Agrawal
Deputy Director General (Agril. Edn.)

Message

It is with immense pleasure and a sense of purpose that I provide this forward to the National Agricultural Higher Education Project-Institutional Development Plan (NAHEP-IDP) at Dr. Balasaheb Sawant Konkan Krishi Vidyapeeth (DBSKKV) and the concurrent endeavour to develop a short pilot course in skilling small-scale agri-entrepreneurship. This transformative initiative is under the guidance and leadership of the Hon'ble Vice Chancellor of DBSKKV Dr.S.G.Bhave.

Principal Investigator of NAHEP-IDP, DBSKKV-Dapoli Dr. P.S.Bodake, a distinguished and visionary leader in the field of agriculture, has consistently championed the cause of advancing agricultural education, research, and extension services. His strategic vision has played a pivotal role in shaping the trajectory of agricultural development in our nation, with a keen focus on empowering farming communities and fostering innovation.

The NAHEP-IDP of DBSKKV stands as a testament to ICAR & World Bank commitment to elevating the standards of agricultural education. By providing institutional support and promoting excellence across various facets of academia, research, and extension activities, the project aims to position DBSKKV as a center of excellence in agricultural learning and research.

In tandem with the NAHEP-IDP, the initiation of a short pilot course in skilling smallscale agri-entrepreneurship reflects DBSKKV foresight in addressing contemporary challenges in agriculture. Recognizing the pivotal role played by small-scale agri-entrepreneurs in driving rural economies, this course is designed to equip them with the necessary skills and knowledge to navigate the dynamic landscape of agribusiness.

The NAHEP-IDP, DBSKKV envisions this pilot course as a stepping stone toward fostering a culture of entrepreneurship in agriculture. By blending theoretical insights with practical applications, the course seeks to empower agri-entrepreneurs, enabling them to adopt sustainable farming practices, embrace innovation, and contribute significantly to the economic prosperity of their communities.

I extend my heartfelt appreciation to Dr. P.S. Bodake and his entire NAHEP-IDP Team for their steadfast leadership and unwavering commitment to advancing agricultural education and entrepreneurship. Under his guidance, these initiatives are poised to make a lasting impact on the agricultural education landscape and the entrepreneurial spirit within the students and farming community.

(R.C. Agrawal)
Deputy Director General (Agril. Edn.)

DR. BALASAHEB SAWANT KONKAN KRISHI VIDYAPEETH
Dapoli, Dist. Ratnagiri - 415712
Tel. No.: (0)02358-282064, **Fax No.**: 02358-282074, **Mob.**: 9422556565
E-mail : vcdbskkv-mh@gov.in, ipmbhave@gmail.com, **website** : www.dbskkv.org

Dr. Sanjay G. Bhave
IDP Leader
Vice Chancellor, DBSKKV

Message

I am delighted to present the Institutional Development Plan as part of the National Agricultural Higher Education Project (NAHEP) undertaken by our esteemed institution. This initiative marks a significant milestone in our commitment to advancing agricultural education, research, and innovation, with the ultimate goal of transforming the agricultural landscape of our nation.

This pilot course serves as a testament to our university's dedication to fostering innovation and fostering collaboration between academia and industry. We believe that by offering this course, we are not only contributing to the skill development of individuals but also playing a pivotal role in shaping the future of agriculture.

We at DBSKKV are happy to felicitate the proficient attainment of the Principal Investigator, IDP Coordinator, and Dean and Director of Instruction of DBSKKV-Dr.Prashant S. Bodake and team NAHEP-IDP involved in the same vertical. Your magnificent work makes all of us highly gratified and prosperous. Well Done!

I extend my gratitude to the faculty members, industry experts, and stakeholders who have contributed their expertise and insights to the development of this course. Their collective efforts have ensured that the curriculum aligns with the ever-changing demands of the agricultural sector.

I am excited to witness the impact that this short pilot course on skilling small-scale agricultural entrepreneurship will have on our participants and, consequently, on the agricultural landscape. With this initiative, we are sowing the seeds of empowerment and innovation, cultivating a new generation of agripreneurs who will not only navigate challenges but also unearth opportunities for growth.

(Sanjay G. Bhave)
IDP Leader
Vice Chancellor, DBSKKV

NATIONAL AGRICULTURAL HIGHER EDUCATION PROJECT
AGRICULTURAL EDUCATION DIVISION
INDIAN COUNCIL OF AGRICULTURAL RESEARCH
(Department of Agricultural Research and Education
Ministry of Agriculture and Farmers Welfare, Government of India)
Room No. 514, Krishi Anusandhan Bhawan-II, Pusa, New Delhi-110 012

Date : 14.12.2023

Dr. N.K. Jain
National Coordinator (IDP)

Message

It is a matter of great pleasure to learn that Dr. Balasaheb Sawant Konkan Krishi Vidyapeeth, Dapoli has developed short pilot course on “Skilling Small-scale Agri-Entrepreneurship” for the undergraduate students. The efforts made by DBSKKV, Dapoli and the Knowledge Experts is a significant stride towards fostering interdisciplinary learning and preparing students for the evolving landscape of agriculture. Agriculture, the backbone of our nation, is undergoing a transformative phase that demands a comprehensive understanding of not only traditional farming practices but also entrepreneurial skills. In this context, DBSKKV, Dapoli is driven by the vision to equip undergraduate students with the knowledge and skills necessary to navigate the complexities of modern agriculture and contribute to the burgeoning field of agri-entrepreneurship. I commend the leadership of Dr. S.G. Bhave, Hon’ble Vice Chancellor, DBSKVV, Dapoli for his forward-thinking approach in embracing this initiative and commitment to provide a robust academic environment aligns seamlessly with our objective of preparing students for the dynamic and competitive landscape of agriculture and entrepreneurship.

I also congratulate Dr. P.S. Bodake, Principal Investigator of NAHEP-IDP, DBSKKV, Dapoli and his entire team, whose collaborative efforts have been instrumental in shaping the curriculum of this course. Together, we envision a program that not only imparts knowledge but also nurtures a spirit of inquiry and enterprise among the students. I extend my warmest congratulations to the University on the launch of the innovative short pilot course on “Skilling Small-scale Agri-Entrepreneurship”. May this endeavour be a beacon of progress, fostering excellence in agricultural education and empowering the next generation of agri-entrepreneurs. University’s commitment to bridging theory and practical is commendable, and I am confident that this initiative will contribute significantly to the growth of our agricultural landscape.

Place: New Delhi

(N. K. Jain)

NATIONAL AGRICULTURE HIGHER EDUCATION PROJECT INSTITUTIONAL DEVELOPMENT PLAN

DR. BALASAHEB SAWANT KONKAN KRISHI VIDYAPEETH,

DAPOLI, DIST. RATNAGIRI

Mob. No.: 9420413255 / 8275201130

Email.: (P)prameghash@gmail.com (O) hodagrodapoli@gmail.com (O) piidpdbskkv@gmail.com (O)nodalcelldbskkv@gmail.com

Dr. P. S. Bodake
Dean & Director of Instruction
Coordinator, Principal Investigator, NAHEP-IDP

Message

It is with immense pride and anticipation that I present the Institutional Development Plan as part of our active involvement in the National Agricultural Higher Education Project (NAHEP). This plan embodies our institution's unwavering commitment to redefining agricultural education and research, and it signifies a transformative journey towards excellence and innovation.

Through this plan, we aim to enhance our institutional capacities, bolster research initiatives, and cultivate strategic partnerships with industries and communities. By incorporating modern pedagogical techniques, fostering interdisciplinary collaboration, and harnessing the potential of emerging technologies, we strive to create a learning ecosystem that empowers our students to become leaders and change-makers in the agricultural sector and it will not only elevate our institution's stature but also propel the agricultural education and research landscape towards a brighter and more sustainable future.

Our joint commitment to education and empowerment has culminated in the creation of this pilot course. Through a harmonious blend of theoretical insights and practical experiences, participants will delve into market trends, value chain analysis, sustainable practices, financial management, and the integration of technology into agriculture. This holistic approach is designed to prepare individuals to navigate the intricacies of agripreneurship with confidence.

This pilot course is an embodiment of our dedication to fostering collaboration between academia and industry. By bridging the gap between theory and practice, we aim to nurture a new generation of agripreneurs who are poised to steer the agricultural sector towards innovation and growth.

We sincerely mention primitive gratitude towards the former Vice-chancellor of DBSKKV Dr. Sanjay D. Sawant and Vice-chancellor of DBSKKV Dr. Sanjay G. Bhave for such prudent leadership and providence. We feel proud to highlight the sheer hard work and great dedication of the Co-Principal Investigator of NAHEP-IDP and IDP Staff.

We are grateful to the Director of Jamnalal Bajaj Institute of Management-Mumbai Dr. Shrinivasan Iyengar for such excellent association and cordial congruence in the course of developing a short pilot course in skilling small-scale Agri-Entrepreneurship. We also express our sincere gratitude to the faculty members of JBIMS & University of Mumbai, industry experts, and stakeholders whose expertise and contributions have shaped this course. Their collective wisdom ensures that the curriculum remains attuned to the evolving demands of the agricultural landscape.

Thank you.

(P. S. Bodake)
Dean & Director of Instruction
Coordinator, Principal Investigator, NAHEP-IDP

Preface

Information Technology (IT) is increasingly being used in agriculture to improve efficiency and productivity, as well as to help farmers make better decisions about their crops and livestock. One way that IT is being used in agriculture is through precision agriculture. Information and communication technology in agriculture (ICT in agriculture), also known as e-agriculture, focuses on the enhancement of agricultural and rural development through improved information and communication processes. ICT plays a vital role in developing the rural area in various sector, it has helped to develop the rural sector in tremendous way. It is used in rural area for the growth of various fields like education, agriculture, medical treatment and many others.

The agriculture sector in India remains the backbone of its society, employing ~58% of the population. With only 4% of the world's water resources and 2.4% of the world's land, India supports 17.8% of the world's population and 15% of the livestock population. The most important aspect of the agriculture industry may be that it is the source of the world's food supply. Considering that agriculture is responsible for everything from harvesting crops to raising livestock, the agriculture industry meets the daily food needs of vegetarians and carnivores alike.

Internet of Things (IoT) smart agriculture products are designed to help monitor crop fields using sensors and by automating irrigation systems. As a result, farmers and associated brands can easily monitor the field conditions from anywhere without any hassle. The authors specified Some of the applications of AI and IoT in Agriculture are in the areas of Precision Farming, Agricultural Drones and Hopping systems, Livestock Monitoring, Monitor Climate Conditions, Smart Greenhouses, AI and IoT based Computer imaging etc.

The entire book is divided into seven chapter, chapter one is given a basic ideas about the information technology and its significant role, the second one is little bit more emphasize on History of 'e-agriculture' and the Community, the third one is based on Sustainable Agriculture and its components, fourth one is CASE STUDY – EASYKRISHI, fifth is more advanced technological tools on Information Technology(IT) for Agriculture, six is on Applicability of IoT in Agriculture, and finally seventh is specified the cloud computing environment and its usage for agriculture.

Authors

Contents

1

Need of Information Technology in Agriculture

Technology spurs Agricultural productivity through various scientific methods and innovations which is evidenced by the success of the Green revolution leading to agricultural development.

The Green Revolution arrived in India in 1968 and had a remarkable impact on the world of agriculture by increasing production yield by 2.5 times, amounting to approximately 2 billion tones, which has been noted as the world's highest growth rate in the agriculture sector. Because of the science and technologies used in the form of

1. Efficient land use,
2. Seeds of high yielding varieties
3. Two or three crop farming as opposed to single crop farming.
4. The need to meet the needs of a growing market for agricultural products, which should be kept up to date by constantly evolving agricultural technologies.
5. Timely information generation and delivering it to farmers.

Example

1. In 1943, Bengal region had faced the disastrous natural calamity in the form of famine, because of which 4 million people had to lose their lives due to food scarcity. It is the most dangerous famine the world has ever noticed.
2. Orissa floods also reported a similar calamity.

Information technology has the potential to bridge this communication gap. We could have mitigated the damage if we had known about these disasters ahead of time through a pre-event detection system. This technology is being developed, and scientists have created a pre-tsunami detection system that alerts people to the possibility of a tsunami. Quality information has the potential to improve efficiency in all areas of agriculture.

This is also true in the agricultural sector. Farmers require crop information at various stages, such as deciding, seeding, preparing and planting, growing, harvesting, packing and storing, and selling crops. Farmers can obtain information from weather forecasts to pricing with the help of technology, so they can get accurate information about various technologies and crops, which could help in increased agricultural productivity and be beneficial to everyone on the supply chain, from farmers to consumers.

1.1 Challenges

The world's population has increased at an astonishing rate, from 4.4 billion to 6 billion between 1980 and 2000, and to 7 billion by 2015, despite limited natural resources and sustainable food security. Food for all presents a significant challenge to overcome. However, it is being overcome by the application of developed agricultural technologies in a variety of fields.

1.2 Technology in various ways

To satisfy the agricultural needs of a growing population, technologies are developed in various agriculture fields.

1. Horticulture
2. Sericulture
3. Floriculture

Horticulture

Horticulture is the science, technology, and business involved in intensive plant cultivation for human use.

It incorporates

1. Plants for food (fruits, vegetables, mushrooms, culinary herbs)
2. Plants for non-food crops (flowers, trees and shrubs, turf-grass, hops, medicinal herbs).

This range of food, medicinal, environmental, and social products and services are all fundamental to developing and maintaining human health and well-being.

1.3 Technologies in Horticulture

A range of innovative technologies are adapted to improve profitability of horticulture production. Reducing post harvest losses with the implementation of coolbot (Cold and dry storage)

1.4 Postharvest losses

In much of the developing world, rates of postharvest loss exceed 50 percent, and cold storage is virtually non-existentdue to the high cost of equipment and limited electricity. Quickly cooling produce after harvest extends shelf life by reducing metabolic activity, water loss and microbial growth. Farmers who can store their produce longer can access better prices, as market price fluctuates for which **Coolbot** is introduced for the following advantages. It

1. Converts an insulated room and an inexpensive, readily available window air conditioner into a cool room.
    a) Substantially reduces the cost of cool storage for horticultural produce.
    b) Overrides the air conditioners temperature gauge, maximizing cooling power.
2. Makes cold storage a viable option for developing-world farmers, cooperatives and market groups to increase their competitiveness.

1.5 Insect pest damage

Insect pests reduce yields directly by attacking crops and indirectly by transmitting viral diseases. As a result, farmers sell damaged produce or use high levels of pesticides, which can be dangerous to both farmers and consumers. Small-scale growers rarely have access to training on effective pesticide use or alternative methods of pest control, such as integrated pest management. Also the Pest-exclusion nets are used. It

1. Provide an inexpensive, reusable and safe method of managing insect pests.
2. Create a barrier that protects vegetables against pests and associated viral diseases, and improves temperature, light, relative humidity and soil moisture.
3. Increase yields and improve vegetable quality, while reducing the reliance on pesticides that impact environmental and human health.
    a) Are produced locally by mosquito net factories.
4. Increase market opportunities for domestically produced textiles.

Overcoming the challenge of **poor seed** quality implementing **drying beads** that:

1. Provide a widely adaptable method for drying seeds and are reusable.
2. Maintain high seed quality during storage.
3. Lead to higher germination rates and increased yield capacity.

4. Increase farmer incentive to invest in improved cultivars.
5. Can be integrated with local seed systems to increase market for local and improved cultivars.

1.6 Floriculture

Floriculture, or flower farming, is a discipline of horticulture concerned with the cultivation of flowering and ornamental plants for gardens and for floristry, comprising the floral industry

Technologies used:

1. Nursery, Landscaping and Greenhouse technology
2. Worldwide events information
3. A complete production capsule to farmers for large scale cultivation

1.7 Sericulture

Sericulture, or silk farming, is the rearing of silkworms for the production of silk.

Stages of production

The stages of production are as follows:

1. The silk moth lays thousands of eggs.
2. These eggs hatch, and the larvae feed on the mulberry leaves.
3. When the silkworms are about 10,000 times heavier than when they hatched, they are now ready to spin a cocoon.
4. The silk is produced in two glands in the silkworm's head and then forced out in liquid form through the spinnerets.
5. The silk solidifies when it comes in contact with the air.
6. The silkworm spins approximately 1 mile of filament and completely encloses itself in a cocoon in about two or three days but due to quality restrictions; the amount of usable silk in each cocoon is small. As a result, 5500 silkworms are required to produce 1 kg of silk.
7. The silk is obtained from the undamaged cocoons by brushing the cocoon to find the outside end of the filament.
8. The silk filaments are then wound on a reel. One cocoon contains approximately 1,000 yards of silk filament. The silk at this stage is known as raw silk. One thread consists of up to 48 individual silk filaments.

1.8 Technology used

Rearing house

1. A separate house is ideal for silkworm rearing.
2. The rearing house should have enough windows to allow for cross ventilation.
3. To ensure proper disinfection, it should be made airtight.
4. The rearing house must be constructed in such a way that it provides optimal temperature of 26-28 °C and RH of 60-70% for silkworm growth while requiring the least amount of maintenance.
5. Temperature controllers and effective design are used to meet these conditions.

Mulberry Cultivation

Because silkworm larvae feed on mulberry leaves, it is critical that sufficient quantities are produced to meet demand, as 5500 silkworms lay only 1 kg of silk per month. As a result, massive amounts of good mulberry cultivation are required, with pesticides and fertilizers used for nutrient management and good production.

Reeling

A servicing swelling agent called strongly alkaline electrolyzed water (SAEW) was used to silk reels made from Bombyx Mori silkworm cocoons. To create SAEW with a pH of 11.50, tap water was electrolyzed in a combined water electrolyze produced in the lab. While the quantities of Na+ in SAEW were 18% greater than those in the tap water, the hardness of SAEW was 30% lower than that of the tap water. In an airtight container, the SAEW's pH remained constant for at least one month. The classic reeling method (TRM), where penetration is achieved by repeatedly alternating high and low temperatures, was replaced with a 15-minute immersion in pH 11.50 SAEW that included shaking. The enlarged cocoons were put into new pH 11.50 SAEW for reeling at the same temperature or a little lower. The servicing loss from the entire cocoon in pH 11.50 SAEW is around 3.5%, and the single silk fibroin filament's tensile quality is on par with or superior than TRM's. A single step of cocoon swelling in pH 11.50 SAEW (70°C) is all that is required for silk reeling in SAEW, replacing several intricate procedures including water penetration, water absorption, swelling, and finally silk reeling in the TRM.

Twisting

Prior to weaving, the raw silk is boiled in water to remove any remaining gum, then dyed and bleached before being woven into the garment - typically on a handloom. The woven cloth may be dyed and bleached in some cases.

1.9 Role of IT in Agriculture

In the context of agriculture, the potential of information technology (IT) can be assessed broadly under two heads:

1. As a tool for direct contribution to agricultural productivity and
2. As an indirect tool for empowering farmers to make informed and quality decisions which will have a positive impact on the way agriculture and allied activities are conducted.

Precision farming, which is popular in developed countries, makes extensive use of IT to directly contribute to agricultural productivity. To increase agricultural output, remote sensing techniques such as satellite technology, geographic information systems, agronomy, and soil sciences are used. This method is capital intensive and useful when dealing with large tracts of land. As a result, it is better suited for farming on corporate lines. The indirect benefits of IT in empowering Indian farmers are substantial and have yet to be fully realized. The Indian farmer urgently requires timely and dependable information inputs to make decisions. At the moment, farmers rely on the slow and unreliable trickling down of decision inputs from traditional sources. The changing environment faced by Indian farmers makes information not merely useful, but necessary to remain competitive.

1.10 Precision Farming

Precision agriculture (PA) is a farming management strategy that focuses on observing, measuring, and responding to temporal and spatial variability in order to improve the sustainability of agricultural production. It is used in crop production as well as livestock production. Precision agriculture frequently makes use of technologies to automate agricultural operations, improving diagnosis, decision-making, and performance. The late 1980s saw the first conceptual work on PA and practical applications. Precision agriculture research aims to define a decision support system (DSS) for whole farm management with the goal of optimizing input returns while conserving resources.

The development of GPS and Glonass has made precision farming possible. The creation of maps of the spatial variability of as many variables as can be measured (for example, crop yield, terrain features/topography, organic matter content, moisture levels, nitrogen levels, pH, EC, Mg, K, and others) is made possible by the farmer's and/or researcher's ability to pinpoint their exact location in a field. Similar information is gathered by sensor arrays mounted on combine harvesters using GPS. These arrays are made up of multispectral imaging and real-time sensors that monitor everything from plant water status to chlorophyll levels. In order to distribute resources as efficiently as possible, variable rate technology (VRT), which includes seeders, sprayers, etc., uses this data along with satellite imagery.

However, recent technological advances have enabled the use of real-time sensors directly in soil, which can wirelessly transmit data without the Precision agriculture has also been made possible by unmanned aerial vehicles, which are relatively cheap and can be operated by inexperienced pilots. These agricultural drones can be outfitted with multispectral or RGB cameras to capture a large number of images of a field, which can then be stitched together using photogrammetric methods to create orthophotos. In addition to the traditional red, green, and blue values, these multispectral images contain near infrared and red-edge spectrum values, which are used to process and analyze vegetative indexes such as NDVI maps. These drones can capture imagery as well as provide additional geographical references such as elevation, allowing software to perform map algebra functions to create precise topographic maps. These topographic maps can be used to correlate crop health with topography, allowing crop inputs such as water, fertilizer, or chemicals such as herbicides and growth regulators to be optimized through variable rate applications.

1.11 Remote Sensing

Remote sensing is the process of detecting and monitoring an area's physical characteristics from a distance by measuring its reflected and emitted radiation (typically from satellite or aircraft). Remotely sensed images are collected by special cameras, allowing researchers to "sense" things about the Earth.

Passive and active remote sensing are the two basic categories of remote sensing. Natural radiation that is emitted or reflected by the object or its surroundings is picked up by passive sensors. The most frequent source of radiation detected by passive sensors is reflected sunlight. The use of radiometers, charge-coupled devices, infrared, and film cameras are a few examples of passive remote sensors. A sensor then detects and analyzes the radiation that is reflected or backscattered from the target. Active collection, on the other hand, emits energy to scan objects and spaces. The location, speed, and direction of an object are determined by measuring the time delay between emission and return, as in the case of RADAR and LiDAR.

Remote sensing allows for the collection of data on dangerous or inaccessible areas. Monitoring deforestation in areas such as the Amazon Basin, glacial features in the Arctic and Antarctic regions, and depth sounding of coastal and ocean depths are all examples of remote sensing applications. During the Cold War, military collection relied on stand-off data collection about dangerous border areas. Remote sensing also replaces costly and time-consuming data collection on the ground, ensuring that areas or objects are not disturbed in the process.

Remote sensing makes it possible to cover very wide areas, allowing for regional surveys on various topics and the detection of very huge features. It permits repetitive coverage, which is helpful when gathering information on dynamic themes like water, agricultural fields, and other such areas. It also makes it simple to gather data at various scales and resolutions. It is possible to analyse and understand a single image obtained through remote sensing for usage in a variety of applications and objectives. The amount of data that can be obtained from a single remotely sensed image is not constrained. A computer can quickly collect and interpret remotely sensed data, which may then be used for a variety of tasks.

1.12 Geographic Information System (GIS)

A **geographic information system (GIS)** is a tool used to collect, manage, alter, analyze, and display many kinds of geographic data. It is a particular kind of database that combines software tools for managing, analyzing, and visualizing geographic data with that type of database. GIS can assist people and organizations in better understanding geographical patterns and relationships by connecting seemingly unconnected data.

A GIS can be compared to a system since it creates and "manipulates" spatial areas digitally, which may be jurisdictional, functional, or application-specific. A GIS is typically created specifically for an organization. Therefore, a GIS created for one application, jurisdiction, business, or purpose may not be inherently interoperable or compatible with a GIS created for a different application, jurisdiction, business, or purpose. A spatial data architecture, which has no such constrained parameters, is what goes beyond a GIS.

In a broad sense, the term refers to any information system that integrates, stores, edits, analyses, distributes, and displays geographic data in order to inform decision making. GIS applications are tools that enable users to create interactive queries (user-created searches), analyze spatial data, edit data in maps, and visualize the results of these operations. The science underlying geographic concepts, applications, and systems is known as geographic information science.

1.13 Agronomy

Agronomy is the study and application of plants for food, fuel, fiber, and reclamation. Agronomy includes research in plant genetics, plant physiology, meteorology, and soil science. Agronomy is the application of science disciplines such as biology, chemistry, economics, ecology, earth science, and genetics. Agronomists today are involved in a variety of issues, including the production of food, the development of healthier foods, the management of agriculture's environmental impact, and the generation of energy from plants. Crop rotation, irrigation and drainage, plant breeding, plant physiology, soil classification, soil fertility, weed control, insect and pest control are all common specializations for agronomists.

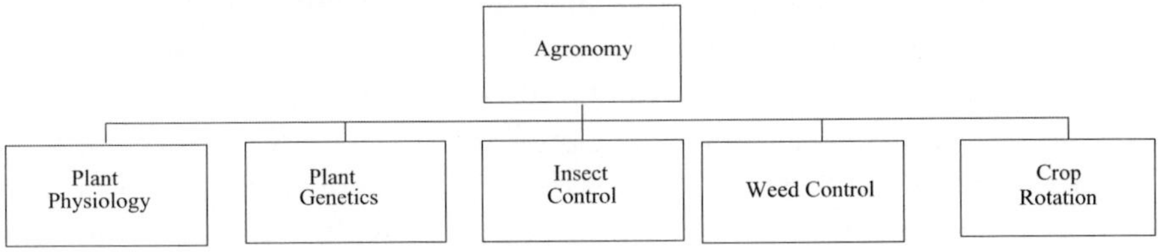

Fig.1.1: Structure of Agronomy

1.14. Soil Sciences

Soil science is the study of soil formation and distribution, biological, chemical, and physical properties and processes, and how these processes interact with larger systems to inform environmental management, industry, and sustainable development.

It is also the study of soils as an environmental resource. Soil science encompasses the following tasks: soil characterization, classification, and mapping, as well as the physical, chemical, hydrologic, mineralogical, biological, and microbiological analysis of soil in general, as well as its assessment, analysis, modeling, testing, evaluation, and use for the benefit of mankind when specifically required to complete the investigation and evaluation of interactions between water, soil, nutrients, plants, and other living organisms.

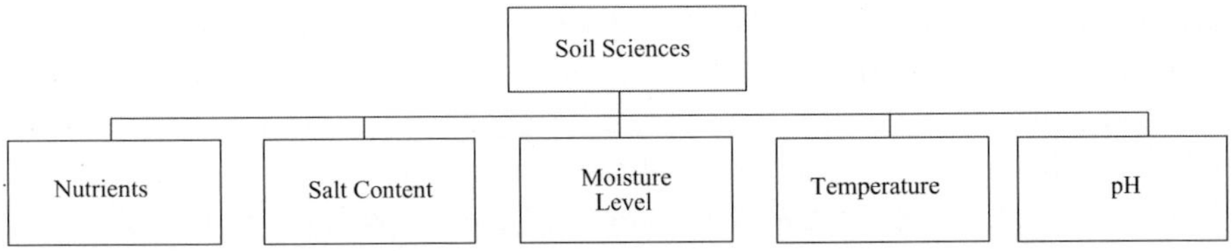

Fig.1.2: Structure of Soil Science

1.15 Other Uses of IT in Agriculture

1. Seeds Development
2. Real time monitoring of temperature variation in storage facilities.
3. Collection of data for crop growth stages via GPS and providing pest information.
4. Weather forecasting.

1.16 Agriculture and Globalization

Globalization of Indian Agriculture C H Hanumantha Rao and Ashok Gulati ('Indian Agriculture: Emerging Perspectives and Policy Issues,' EPW, December 31,1994) have strongly advocated for the integration of Indian agriculture with the global market, arguing that such a process would improve agricultural terms of trade, the benefits of which would trickle down to the poor. To that end, the authors have proposed a strategy for agricultural development that includes broad policy changes in supply side factors and a shift from foodgrain production to new activities with favorable domestic and export demand, such as dairying and other animal products, horticulture, and floriculture, in order to boost agro-processing. Their view is based on the premise that growth rate in domestic demand for food grains has been declining and may not exceed the long-term foodgrain output growth rate of 2.6 per cent per annum due basically to the availability of a wide range of non- food grains and urban consumption goods in rural areas and, therefore, agricultural growth need not any longer be limited by the goal of self-sufficiency but may benefit from trade so as to raise the overall rate of growth.

This view may be questioned on the ground that the consumption basket of the minority of population might have undergone a change in favor of non-food grains and urban consumption goods but certainly not the consumption basket of the vast majority of rural population which contains mainly cereals and the contents of which are shrinking due to rapid erosion of purchasing power, consequent upon rise in the prices of basic consumption goods. The declining demand for food grains may be partly due to lack of purchasing power in the hands of the majority of the population.

Nearly two-thirds of the rural population consists of small and marginal farmers and landless laborers. Their demand for food is not fully met and they are net purchasers in the market. This vast segment of the rural population cannot participate in the process of globalization of agriculture. Since 'surplus' of food grains may not be real, food self-sufficiency will continue to remain one of the goals of agricultural policy in the face of rising population and increasing demand of the poor.

Agricultural value chains are heterogeneous associations of primary producers and other economic agents who aim at improving performance and economic productivity in the market. They differentiate by their technological structure, size of business, educational level and means of access to information. Exchanging information is critical for stakeholders in agricultural value chains due to its nature, as it is the key element for establishing, developing and managing efforts to improve their competitiveness in local and international markets. Information and Communication Technologies (ICTs) are effective tools and in several cases, also innovative to facilitate the exchange of information in the value chains.

1.17 Global factors influencing ICT Usage

1. Infrastructure for access and ICT affordability, including Internet connectivity in production and commercial areas. For example, in Chile and Peru, only 10-11% (estimated) of the rural population has access to the Internet.
2. Higher concentration and usage of ICTs –up to date and innovative technologies- in sectors with more economic power.
3. The quality and availability of information content.
4. Limitation of the media itself.
5. Individuals' choices and their appropriation of ICTs;
6. Support services and training to develop the "culture of use" of ICT and "information literacy" among chain stakeholders.
7. The potential "virtual" relationship between stakeholders in the food value chain may have a counterproductive effect in the negotiations and relationships that have been based on trust and face to face interaction (cultural factors).

1.18 The e-Agriculture Community

1. E-Agriculture is a global **Community of Practice**, where people from all over the world exchange information, ideas, and resources related to the use of information and communication technologies (ICT) for sustainable agriculture and rural development.
2. With over **10,000 members from 160 countries and territories**, the e-Agriculture Community is made up of individual stakeholders such as information and communication specialists, researchers, farmers, students, policy makers, business people, development practitioners, and others.

3. The members have a common interest that brings us together: improving policies and processes around the use of ICT in support of agriculture and rural development, in order to have a positive impact on rural livelihoods.

Mission

Their mission is to act as a catalyst for institutions and individuals working in agricultural and rural development to exchange knowledge, learn from others, and make better decisions regarding the critical role that ICTs play in empowering rural populations, enhancing rural livelihoods, and establishing sustainable agriculture and food security.

How and why do they do it?

They collaborate with partners all across the world to do this. Knowledge sharing between UN agencies, governments, universities, research organizations, NGOs, farmers' organizations, the commercial sector, and the general public is at the heart of e-agriculture. We understand that the most basic definition of knowledge exchange is the beginning of a fruitful conversation. The e-Agriculture Forum series is one of the most well-liked activities as a result. The topics are motivated by interest and are organized by partner institutions with expertise in various facets of e-agriculture.

2

The History of 'e-agriculture' and The Community

Although "e-agriculture" and other initiatives to bridge the rural digital divide were already underway around the world, the Community (and the term "e-agriculture") emerged following the World Summits on the Information Society in 2003 and 2005. The WSIS global participants recognized that when addressing the challenges of the digital divide, particularly in the context of rural livelihoods, problems extend beyond technology. It is a multifaceted problem characterized by ineffective knowledge exchange and information content management, as well as a lack of human resources, institutional capacity, and sensitivity to gender and the diverse needs of various groups. With WSIS participants identifying and naming "e-agriculture" as a key action line to address the Millennium Development Goals, the United Nations Food and Agriculture Organization (FAO) was tasked with leading the development and subsequent facilitation activities that would truly engage stakeholders at all levels.

The e-Agriculture Community was founded in 2006 by a group of Founding Partners and officially launched in 2007. Today, the e-Agriculture Community of Practice is still expanding and supporting its members as well as the communities with which they interact on a daily basis.

2.1 Precision Agriculture

Precision agriculture aims to optimize field-level management with regard to:

1. Crop science: by matching farming practices more closely to crop needs (e.g. Fertilizer inputs);
2. Environmental protection: by reducing environmental risks and footprint of farming (e.g. Limiting leaching of nitrogen);
3. Economics: by boosting competitiveness through more efficient practices (e.g. improved management of fertilizer usage and other inputs).

Precision agriculture also provides farmers with a wealth of information to:

1. Build up a record of their farm;
2. Improve decision-making;
3. Foster greater traceability
4. Enhance marketing of farm products
5. Improve lease arrangements and relationship with landlords
6. Enhance the inherent quality of farm products (e.g. Protein level in bread-flour wheat)

2.2 Emergence of Precision Farming

Precision agriculture first became popular in the United States in the early 1980s. In 1985, researchers at the University of Minnesota experimented with different lime inputs in crop fields. It was also around this time that grid sampling became popular (applying a fixed grid of one sample per hectare). This technique was used toward the end of the 1980s to generate the first input recommendation maps for fertilizers and pH corrections. Since then, the use of yield sensors developed from new technologies, combined with the introduction of GPS receivers, has gained traction.

Today, such systems cover millions of hectares. In the American Midwest (US), it is associated with mainstream farmers who are attempting to maximize profits by spending money only on areas that require fertilizer. This method enables the farmer to vary the rate of fertilizer applied across the field based on the need identified by GPS guided Grid or Zone Sampling. Fertilizer that would otherwise be spread in areas that do not require it can now be placed in areas that do, maximizing its use. Precision agriculture evolved at different rates around the world. The United States, Canada, and Australia were the forerunners.

The United Kingdom was the first in Europe to follow suit, closely followed by France, where it first appeared in 1997-1998. Argentina is the leading country in Latin America, where it was introduced in the mid-1990s with the assistance of the National Agricultural Technology Institute. Because the current agricultural scenario in Brazil is one of efficient production while protecting the environment, Embrapa established the Brazilian Precision Agriculture Research Network with the goal of knowledge generation, tool and technology development on precision agriculture to soybean, maize, wheat, rice, cotton, pasture, eucalyptus, pines, grapes, peach, orange, and sugar cane crops. The advancement of GPS and variable-rate spreading techniques aided in the establishment of precision farming management practices. Today, variable-rate systems are used by less than 10% of France's farmers. GPS is becoming more popular. However, this has not stopped them from utilizing precision agriculture services, which provide field-level recommendation maps.

Precision agriculture management practices can help farmers use fewer nutrients and other crop inputs while increasing yields. Farmers earn a return on investment by saving money on phytosanitary and fertilizer costs. The second, larger-scale benefit of targeting inputs concerns environmental impacts on a spatial, temporal, and quantitative scale. Applying the right amount of inputs at the right time and place benefits crops, soils, and groundwater, as well as the entire crop cycle. As a result, because it respects crops, soils, and farmers, precision agriculture has become a cornerstone of sustainable agriculture. Sustainable agriculture aims to ensure a continuous supply of food while remaining within the ecological, economic, and social constraints required to sustain production over time. Precision agriculture therefore seeks to use high-tech systems in pursuit of this goal.

2.3 E-Commerce in Agriculture

The US found that farmers were primarily using the Internet to access information on commodity prices, weather, farm chemicals, and machinery. The study also showed that farmers were migrating quickly toward Web-based transactions such as purchasing seed, crop chemicals, and farm equipment on the Internet

Agricultural Information Exchange and Communication

The most frequently encountered e-Agriculture approach relates to improved information exchange and communication for the benefit of rural communities, farm households, and the rural service providers involved in the provision of agricultural, financial and communication services.

1. Egypt VERCON (Virtual Extension and Research Communication Network): Researchers and extension workers presently access information resources such as extension brochures, statistical databases, decision support systems, and can participate in special interest forums, online discussions, news and events. An online query system called Farmer's Problems answers technical questions raised by smallholder farmers.
2. Food Net: This network in Uganda comprises a national system that was established together to disseminate agricultural market price information via newspapers, the Internet, radio and mobile phones (SMS).
3. Rural Radio, ICTs and Food Security: FAO is working with the World Association of Community Broadcasters, AMARC, an international

community radio network, and the Developing Countries' Farm Radio Network (DCFRN) to enhance networking and sharing by assisting radio stations to use the Internet to access alternative information on a range of subjects of interest to rural communities, including health, education, credit and local projects.

2.4 Bridging the Rural Divide

Begun in 2003, the **Food and Agriculture Organization of the United Nations** (FAO) implemented a strategic Programme entitled "Bridging the Rural Digital Divide". The programme highlighted innovative approaches to knowledge exchange that were taking advantage of new (at that time) digital technologies, and that were based on synergies between information management and communication for development. At the time this was referred to as "information and communication for development"(ICD).

The Programme sought to bring relevant expertise and resources across the international development community into a more coherent and systematic approach. Innovators in many parts of the world were already developing initiatives which, if brought together, were believed to have a greater potential than if they remained isolated or fragmented.

2.5 Programme Objectives

1. Increase the availability of information content related to rural areas in digital form.
2. Develop innovative mechanisms and processes for information exchange and communication.
3. Establish networks and communities of practice in information and communication for development and for exchange of information on agriculture and rural development.
4. The conceptual basis for the programme was devised through a range of background studies that drew particularly on concepts embodied in livelihoods approaches* to sustainable development. An important consideration of the programme was to support the links from macro level (policies and institutions) to micro level (communities and individuals).

A set of key determinants for the successful application of ICT which will guide the Programme are:

1. Locally-adapted content and context
2. Building on existing systems
3. Addressing diversity

4. Building capacity
5. Access, empowerment and democratization
6. Strengthening partnerships
7. Realistic approaches to technologies to support information and communication Information costs, value and financial sustainability

2.6 Genetically Modified Crops

Genetically modified crops (**GMCs**, **GM crops**, or **biotech crops**) are plants, the DNA of which has been modified using genetic engineering techniques. In most cases the aim is to introduce a new trait to the plant which does not occur naturally in the species. Examples include resistance to certain pests, diseases, or environmental conditions, or resistance to chemical treatments (e.g. resistance to an herbicide), or the production of a certain nutrient or pharmaceutical agent.

Genetic engineering techniques are much more precise than mutagenesis (mutation breeding) where an organism is exposed to radiation or chemicals to create a non-specific but stable change. Other techniques by which humans modify plants include selective breeding; plant breeding, and somaclonal variation.

There is broad scientific consensus that food on the market derived from GM crops poses no greater risk to human health than conventional food. However, opponents have objected to GM crops per se on several grounds, including environmental concerns, whether food produced from GM crops is safe, whether GM crops are needed to address the world's food needs, and economic concerns raised by the fact these organisms are subject to intellectual property law.

How does Globalization Help?

1. GM or GE crops are the future of Agriculture Science
2. 98.7 million hectares of GM crops grown in 2012
3. 25% of maize grown worldwide is GM
4. 46 % of Soya grown worldwide is GM
5. USA, Australia, Argentina, Bulgaria, Canada, China, Honduras, Mexico, Spain, Uruguay etc are leaders in GM crops
6. Major GM crops in India- Golden rice, cotton, mustard, sugarcane, papaya, castor, soybean, brinjal, rice, tomato etc.

2.7 How does a genetically modified crop gets produced?

Genetic modification refers to techniques used to manipulate the genetic composition of an organism by adding specific useful genes. A gene is a sequence of DNA that contains information that determines a particular characteristic/ trait. All organisms have DNA (genes). Genes are located in chromosomes. Genes are units of inheritance that are passed from one generation to the next and provide instructions for development and function of the organism. Crops that are developed through genetic modification are referred to as genetically modified (GM) crops, transgenic crops or genetically engineered (GE) crops.

The main steps involved in the development of GM crops are:

1. **Isolation of the gene(s) of interest:** Existing knowledge about the structure, function or location on chromosomes is used to identify the gene(s) that is responsible for the desired trait in an organism, for example, drought tolerance or insect resistance.
2. **Insertion of the gene(s) into a transfer vector:** The most commonly used gene transfer tool for plants is a circular molecule of DNA (plasmid) from the naturally occurring soil bacterium, Agrobacterium Tumefactions. The gene(s) of interest is inserted into the plasmid using recombinant DNA (rDNA) techniques. For additional information see Plasmids link
3. **Plant transformation:** The modified A. tumefaciens cells containing the plasmid with the new gene are mixed with plant cells or cut pieces of plants such as leaves or stems (explants). Some of the cells take up a piece of the plasmid known as the T-DNA (transferred-DNA). The A. tumefaciens inserts the desired genes into one of the plant's chromosomes to form GM (or transgenic) cells. The other most commonly used method to transfer DNA is particle bombardment (gene gun) where small particles coated with DNA molecules are bombarded into the cell. For additional information see Plant Transformation using Agro bacterium tumefaciens and Plant Transformation using Particle Bombardment links.
4. **Selection of the modified plant cells:** After transformation, various methods are used to differentiate between the modified plant cells and the great majority of cells that have not incorporated the desired genes. Most often, selectable marker genes that confer antibiotic or herbicide resistance are used to favor growth of the transformed cells relative to the non-transformed cells. For this method, genes responsible for resistance are inserted into the vector and transferred along with the gene(s) conferring desired traits to the plant cells. When the cells are exposed to the antibiotic or herbicide, only the transformed cells (containing and expressing the selectable marker gene) will survive. The transformed cells are then regenerated to form whole plants using tissue culture methods.

5. **Regeneration into whole plants via tissue culture** involves placing the explants (plant parts/cells) onto media containing nutrients that induce development of the cells into various plant parts to form whole plantlets (Figure 1). Once the plantlets are rooted they are transferred to pots and kept under controlled environmental conditions.
6. **Verification of transformation and characterization of the inserted DNA fragment.** Verification of plant transformation involves demonstrating that the gene has been inserted and is inherited normally. Tests are done to determine the number of copies inserted, whether the copies are intact, and whether the insertion does not interfere with other genes to cause unintended effects. Testing of gene expression (i.e., production of messenger RNA and/or protein, evaluation of the trait of interest) is done to make sure that the gene is functional.

The steps are depicted in a diagrammatic manner as shown below:

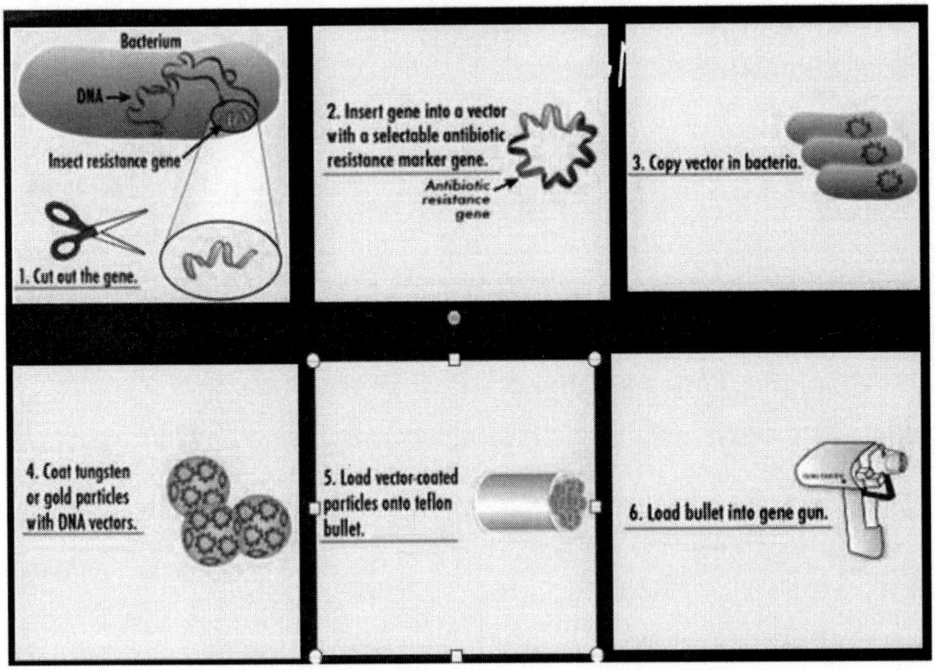

Fig. 2.1: Safety Parameters and Components

7. **Testing of plant performance** is generally carried out first in the greenhouse or screen house to determine whether the modified plant has the desired new trait and does not have any new unwanted characteristics. Those that perform well are planted into the field for further testing. In the field, the plants are first grown in confined field trials to test whether

the technology works (if the plants express the desired traits) in the open environment. If the technology works then the plants are tested in multi-location field trials to establish whether the crop performs well in different environmental conditions. If the GM crop passes all the tests, it may then be considered for commercial production.

8. **Safety assessment.** Food and environmental safety assessment are carried out in conjunction with testing of plant performance.

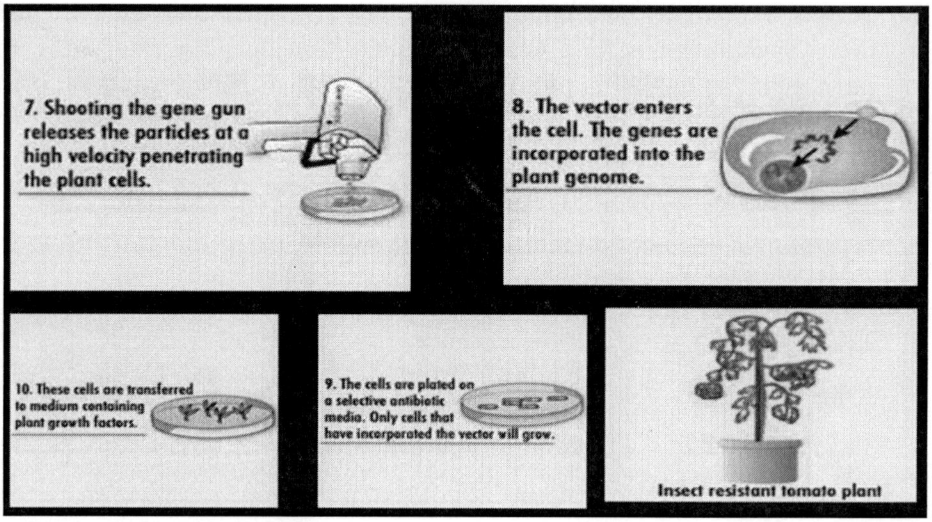

Fig. 2.2: High Velocity Plant Cell

2.8 Changing Pattern of Needs - Post WTO

While relevant information of the required quality always had the potential of improving efficiency in all spheres of activity of Indian farmer, the emerging scenario of a deregulated agriculture, thanks to WTO, has brought in a 'need' and urgency to make it an integral part of decision making. Consequently, deploying IT as a strategic tool for the benefit of rural India has assumed importance. Since information needs of the Indian farmers in general are documented extensively, it is more pertinent to focus on the theme in the context of challenges raised by WTO. The broad information inputs required by farmers in the new scenario can be classified as

i) Awareness Databases - those that facilitate proper understanding of the implications of the WTO on Indian agriculture,

ii) Decision Support Systems - information that facilitates farmers to make a proper SWOT analysis to take appropriate decisions,

iii) Systems that facilitate Indian farmers to forge appropriate alliances for collective benefit,

iv) Information on new opportunities

v) Monitoring systems for corrective measures.

i) **Awareness Databases:** First and foremost, it is essential to provide unambiguous interpretation and implications of WTO for ordinary people. The jargon and the language under various articles of WTO require to be distilled by experts and their implications are clearly to be spelled out for all the segments of Indian agriculture and allied activities. The implications for all the stakeholders and the time frames are to be spelt out. This is a priority item which is to be addressed immediately. The mandatory changes in government policies on tariffs, imports, year wise phasing of the same, and the impact on various subsidy schemes would be of concern to people. An area of immediate concern to farmers is to get an analytical input on how his/her life is going to be affected. Since removal of restrictions throw open Indian agricultural markets, the macro economic situation related to foreign exchange, inflation, the current tariff structure within and outside the country etc. and their likely impact on Indian agriculture will have a direct bearing on the decisions of segments of Indian agriculture.

ii) **Decision Support Systems for farmers:** Indian farmers are cautious and usually tend to avoid risk. It is suggested that the provisions of WTO stipulating reductions in export subsidies on farm products will make Indian exports more competitive. It is estimated that the export potential may touch $ 1.5 billion by 2005. In order to take advantage of the emerging order, the enterprising Indian farmer needs to be equipped with information that facilitates undertaking a proper SWOT analysis and compare it with conventional wisdom and satisfy himself on an appropriate course of action.

The data on cost of cultivation, efficient agricultural practices and availability of inputs will facilitate in assessing the strengths of indigenous products vis a vis the imports. Availability of information on the weaknesses as evident from the adverse effect of WTO on any specific agricultural product will help in taking the necessary corrective measures. In the emerging scenario, competitive advantage is required to be fully exploited to improve export potential. India is believed to have competitive advantage in areas like fruits, oil seeds, cotton, and milk products. Special thrust may be accorded to these sectors to meet international standards. Opportunities for specialization may lead to better export potential.

Similarly, forecasts on threats in terms of information related to cheaper imports, macro-economic conditions of other countries are also required.

iii) **Systems that facilitate Indian farmers to forge appropriate alliances for collective benefit:** The size of land holdings is a major barrier in exploiting any export potential. In order to remain competitive and derive better price realizations, it will be imperative for the farmers to come together through cooperative alliances. It is possible to relieve the farmers of geographical barriers by facilitating farmers to come together online and facilitate disposal of their produce at attractive prices. Online bidding can be introduced for various agricultural product categories. This will require development of complicated IT systems which are to be supported by proper bricks and mortar infrastructure and post harvest technologies, storage, etc.

iv) **Opportunities**: in the new order It is necessary to equip Indian farmers to come together for value additions to their agricultural output. This will get them better returns from their produce and at the same time generate new employment opportunities in the rural sector. This will require systems to provide information to farmers on agro processing industries, aqua culture units, animal husbandry, floriculture, etc. The opportunities for setting up such units, procedures related to exports, the quality norms to be adopted, packaging, etc.

v) **Monitoring:** Since the domestic agricultural scene is exposed to international fluctuations, it is necessary to be vigilant to external shocks. Systems to monitor international market status, international supply - demand scenario, macro economic factors, political disruptions are required to be developed. Advance warning systems to alert the farmers are required to be developed. It is necessary to promote monitoring cells in all major institutions related to agriculture and allied activities to maintain data, provide periodic analytical reports and raise advance alerts.

2.9 IT and Indian Agriculture in the Future

Technologically it is possible to develop suitable systems, as outlined in the previous sections, to cater to the information needs of Indian farmers. User friendly systems, particularly with content in local languages, can generate interest in the farmers and others working at the grassroots. It is possible to create dedicated networks or harness the power of the Internet to make these services available to all parts of the country. The task of creating application packages and databases to cater to the complete spectrum of Indian agriculture is a giant task. The Long Term Agriculture Policy provides an exhaustive list of all the areas that are to be covered. This can be taken as a guiding list to evolve design and develop suitable systems catering to each of the specified areas. Our country has the advantage of having a large number of specialized institutions in place catering to various aspects of Indian agriculture.

These institutions can play a crucial role in designing the necessary applications & databases and services. This will facilitate modularization of the task, better control and help in achieving quick results. As it is, several institutions have already developed systems related to their area of specialization. For quick results, it may be useful to get the applications outsourced to software companies in India. This will facilitate quick deployment of applications and provide a boost to the software industry in India. In order to avoid duplication of efforts, it may be useful to consider promoting a coordinating agency which will have an advisory role to play in evolving standard interface for users, broad design and monitoring of the progress.

In the post WTO regime, it is suggested that it is useful to focus more on some agricultural products to maintain an unquestionable competitive advantage for exports. This will call for urgent measures to introduce state of the art technologies such as remote sensing, geographical information systems (GIS), bio-engineering, etc. India has made rapid strides in satellite technologies. It is possible to effectively monitor agricultural performance using remote sensing and GIS applications. This will not only help in planning, advising and monitoring the status of the crops but also will help in responding quickly to crop stress conditions and natural calamities. Challenges of crop stress, soil problems, and natural disasters can be tackled effectively through these technologies.

A beginning in precision farming can be encouraged in larger tracts of land in which export potential can be tilted in our country's favor. While developing these systems it is necessary to appreciate that major audience that is targeted is not comfortable with computers. This places a premium on user friendliness and it may be useful to consider touch screen technologies to improve user comfort levels. It is often observed that touch screen kiosks, with their intuitive approach, provide a means for quick learning and higher participation. It is also necessary to provide as much content as possible in local languages.

Once the required application packages & databases are in place, a major challenge is with respect to dissemination of the information. The Krishi Vigyan Kendra, NGOs and cooperative societies may be used to set up information kiosks. Private enterprise is also required to be drawn into these activities. These kiosks should provide information on other areas of interest such as education, information for which people have to travel distances such as those related to the government, courts, etc. Facilities for email, raising queries to experts, uploading digital clips to draw the attention of experts to location specific problems can be envisaged.

2.10 Constraints and Remedies for Effective Dissemination

Some of the major constraints delaying the spread of e-revolution to rural India are listed below :

1. **Haphazard development :** It is observed that some initiatives have already been made to provide IT based services to rural communities. However, duplication of efforts are witnessed as most of the services revolve around limited subjects. Keeping in view the giant task involved, it is necessary to form a coordination mechanism to strive for a concerted effort to support the farming community in the country. Such a coordination agency may only have advisory powers such as user interface, broad design, delivery mechanism of the content, standards for setting up kiosks.
2. **User friendliness:** The success of this strategy depends on the ease with which rural the population can use the content. This will require intuitive graphics based presentation. Touch screen kiosks are required to be set up to encourage greater participation
3. **Local languages:** Regional language fonts and mechanisms for synchronization of the content provides a challenge that needs to be met with careful planning.
4. **Restrictions:** Information content based on remote sensing and geographical information systems can provide timely alerts to the farmers and also improve the efficiency of administration. These applications can have a major impact on the farmers and help them to appreciate the potential of information technology. However, government's map restriction policies often threaten to stifle the optimal utilization of these tools.
5. **Power supply:** In most of rural India, power supply is not available for long hours. This will reduce the usefulness of the intended services. Since almost the entire country receives sunshine for most part of the year, it is useful to explore solar power packs for UPS as well as for supply of power. The Ministry of Non-conventional Energy Sources may pay special attention in this area which can be a major contributor to the growth of IT in villages.
6. **Connectivity:** Despite the phenomenal progress made in the recent years, the connectivity to rural areas still requires improvement . Reliable connectivity is a prerequisite for a successful penetration of IT into rural

areas. Many private ISPs are setting up large networks connecting many major towns and cities. Since some of these networks pass through rural areas, it is possible to provide connectivity to a large number of villages. Several technologies exist that can be utilized for connecting rural areas. Cable network is a possible medium for providing the last mile connectivity to villages.

7. **Bandwidth:** Even in areas where telephone and other communication services exist, the available bandwidth is a major constraint. Since internet based rural services require substantial use of graphics, low bandwidth is one of the major limitations in providing effective e-services to farmers. As already stated, networks with high bandwidth are being set up by several companies passing through rural segments which can be utilized. Until this materializes, a two pronged strategy of storing static information at the kiosks and providing dynamic information from remote locations can be examined. The graphic oriented content which does not change frequently, such as, demonstration clips for farmers, can be stored on the local drives at the kiosks and arrange for periodic updating of this information over the network during non-peak hours. The dynamic information which changes more frequently can be accessed from remote locations to obtain the latest status.
8. **Dissemination points:** Mass deployment of information kiosks is critical for effective use of the Internet based content and services. In order to ensure that the information kiosks are economically feasible, it is necessary to make the proposition sustainable and viable. This requires a major focus on a viable revenue model for such kiosks. In the new information era, the kiosks should be designed to become electronic super markets that can, in addition to being information sources, handle other services of use to the people living in rural areas. The revenue available through such sources can make a kiosk attractive for prospective investors.

The Government can provide finance facilities to unemployed rural agricultural graduates who can be expected to have greater commitment and at the same time act as an efficient interface for less educated rural visitors. The objective should be to transform rural information kiosks into 'clicks and mortar' gateway to rural India for 'Bricks and mortar' industry. Some of the sources that can generate revenue for rural kiosks are :

a) **Distance education** - A large number of people travel substantial distances to attend educational courses. It is possible to set up virtual classrooms right in their villages

b) **Training** - People living in rural areas require training and a means for upgrading their skills in their area of work. It is possible to provide quality education right at their door steps with facilities for online interaction with experts. For example, a village teacher or a paramedical staff can keep abreast latest developments without disturbing his/her routine. Similarly, training can be imparted on various aspects of agriculture such as correct practices, irrigation practices, efficient utilization of tools used in farming such as tractors.

c) **Insurance** : The advent of private players into insurance has brought about advanced IT systems that can render services over networks. The kiosks can be insurance agents for insurance firms which, in turn, can compensate the kiosk operators for online transactions for new business as well as maintaining the old.

d) **Local agent** : Many companies have difficulty in working out logistics for their supplies to rural outlets. A rural kiosk can act as conduit for such 'bricks and mortar' companies. This has the potential of transforming a rural kiosk into a profitable venture.

e) **Rural post office** : The kiosks can facilitate sending and receiving emails, facilitate 'chats' with experts. Several successful rural kiosks are already available in many states which run essentially on this model.

f) **e-Governance** : Rural kiosks are the stepping stones for effective implementation of e-governance. Details related to central / state / local governments, formats and procedures, status verification such as case listings in courts, filing of applications in electronic format where admissible, etc. are some of the areas where kiosks can be of major use.

g) **Online examinations** : Online certification examinations are 'in things' with many organizations and certification agencies. Many people are forced to stay at metros to take the examinations. Eventually it should be possible to conduct these examinations through the rural kiosks.

The Directorate of Marketing and Inspection (DMI), part of the Ministry of Agriculture and the Government of India, sanctioned the Agricultural Marketing Information Network (AGMARKNET) project to be implemented by National Informatics Centre (NIC). Launched in March 2000, it aims to link all important agricultural produce markets spread across the subcontinent with the State Agricultural Marketing Boards and Directorates for effective information exchange.

A step towards globalization of Indian agriculture, the NIC-based, e-governance portal AGMARKNET facilitates generation and transmission of prices, commodity arrival information from agricultural produce markets, and Web-based dissemination to producers, consumers, traders, and policy makers transparently and quickly. AGMARKNET aims at improving the decision-making capability of the farmers and strengthening their bargaining power.

Situation

India has an expanding population of one billion to feed and over 70 percent of its national workforce is directly or indirectly dependent on agriculture. The agricultural sector has been successful over the past four decades, in keeping pace with the rising demand for food. Agricultural marketing is an area for the "second generation" of green revolution problems. Indian marketing is undergoing a significant metamorphosis because of economic liberalization and globalization.

To fully utilize the new emerging trade opportunities for the benefit of farming community, the Department of Agriculture and Cooperation, in the Ministry of Agriculture sanctioned an Information, Communication and Technology (ICT) based central sector scheme, Agricultural Marketing Information Network (AGMARKNET). Commenting on the need for an online marketplace, Shared Joshi, Former Chairman, High Level Task Force on Agriculture (2000), Government of India said, "It is advantageous to have a network down to the mandi level to begin with. This can be progressively extended to villages and household level in due course of time."

AGMARKNET ensures dissemination of data through the network to any distance for the benefit of citizens, farmers, traders, and consumers. The improved communication system will enable producers to learn about probable markets in which their produce can be disposed of more profitably. Also the modernization of the market information system will lead to efficiency in markets and increased participation of the farmers.

The AGMARKNET portal is constantly enriched with agricultural marketing–related information. Efforts are on to reach out to the farmers in their regional languages. As of now, the portal is disseminating information in two regional languages: Hindi and Punjabi. The portal also caters to the diversified needs of these stakeholders by providing the following agricultural marketing–related information as a single window Web service over the Internet.

Price and Arrivals

The portal provides access to commodity-wise, variety-wise daily prices and arrivals information of various wholesale markets. Future prices from national multi-commodity exchanges are reflected online. Also linkages are established with Web sites of the FAO and Asia & Pacific Coconut Community (APCC) to access international commodity price trends.

Commodities and Varieties

A commodity base, comprising more than 300 commodities and about 2,000 varieties has been evolved. The commodities are being categorized into various groups: cereals, pulses, oil seeds, fruits, vegetables, spices, fiber crops, beverages, forest products, drugs and narcotics, dry fruits, flowers, forest products, livestock/poultry, and so forth to facilitate easy retrieval of market information.

Grading and Standardization

To promote the importance of quality among the farming community, the portal emphasizes on standardization and grading aspects of the agricultural products. The information is provided in the form of documents/specifications prescribed by the act/rules of DMI and other agencies. It also links to the Codex International food standards, guidelines, and related texts such as the codes of practice under the joint FAO/World Health Organization (WHO) Food Standards Program.

Market Atlas

The market profiles and various Geographical Information System (GIS)-based thematic maps are under development.

2.11 E-Directory of Markets

With the networking of agricultural markets, timely and effective exchange of information electronically is now possible. E-mail addresses of the agencies involved are progressively published for public access so as to facilitate direct interaction.

Benefits

The AGMARKNET project has strengthened the interfaces among government organizations, farmers, industry, policy makers, and other beneficiaries. "The project aims at empowering the farming community with market information. For maximizing the benefits it needs to be integrated with other ICT initiatives targeting the upliftment of rural India. The project is part of the National e-Government action plan of the Government of India.

Efficient and timely utilization of market data

Agmarknet has helped establish a nationwide information network for speedy collection and dissemination of market data for efficient and timely utilization. AGMARKNET Programme plays a catalytic role for ushering in "market-led agricultural extension" in India, highly scalable, planned through bottom-up process, and implemented through active involvement and collaboration of agricultural market committees in India."

Farmer empowerment

"The AGMARKNET has already emerged as the sun-shine website to bargain better prices for their produce, and marching ahead towards becoming an e-Commerce and e-Business Portal in India,"

Price transparency

The speedier collection and dissemination of information on commodities enables farmers to realize better prices. This also leads to transparency in the pricing process across the country. Progressive sensitization and orientation of farmers helps them respond to new challenges in agricultural marketing by using Information, Communication and Technology (ICT) as a vehicle of extension. "This "digital development in rural areas" of India facilitates rural prosperity, rural empowerment, and a warehousing of "data for development" – a step towards digital inclusion to foster rural enterprise in India,"

Reports on prices & arrivals

1. Commodity-wise, Market-wise Daily Report
2. Market-wise, Commodity-wise Daily Report
3. Commodity Prices during last week
4. Market-wise Prices during last week
5. Commodity Transactions Below MSP
6. Commodity-wise, Market-wise Daily Report for a State
7. Date wise Prices for Specified commodity
8. State wise, Market-wise, Commodity-wise Daily Report

2.12 Associated Challenges & Roll-out issues

1. Markets in remote rural areas, erratic power supply, non-availability of infrastructure, frequent transfers of market personnel trained for reporting data, non-transparent auctions in markets

2. Inconsistent reporting and data quality issues in certain cases. Because of the multi-layered system, Ownership by States is not by default; constant monitoring and persuasion at various levels needed in the present system to ensure regular, reliable and consistent information flow as Agricultural markets are autonomous bodies.

3

Sustainable Agriculture

The goal of sustainable agriculture is to meet society's food and textile needs in the present without compromising the ability of future generations to meet their own needs.

Practitioners of sustainable agriculture seek to integrate three main objectives into their work: a healthy environment, economic profitability, and social and economic equity. Every person involved in the food system—growers, food processors, distributors, retailers, consumers, and waste managers—can play a role in ensuring a sustainable agricultural system.

3.1 FPO Problems

There are many practices commonly used by people working in sustainable agriculture and sustainable food systems. Growers may use methods to promote soil health, minimize water use, and lower pollution levels on the farm. Consumers and retailers concerned with sustainability can look for "values-based" foods that are grown using methods promoting farm worker wellbeing, that are environmentally friendly, or that strengthen the local economy. And researchers in sustainable agriculture often cross disciplinary lines with their work: combining biology, economics, engineering, chemistry, community development, and many others. However, sustainable agriculture is more than a collection of practices. It is also process of negotiation: a push and pull between the sometimes competing interests of an individual farmer or of people in a community as they work to solve complex problems about how we grow our food and fiber.

It has been observed that the FPOs perform better when its management systems, governance and capital structure are strong. Other factors like market and financial accessibility, farmer-members engagement plan, infrastructure development, etc. should also be strengthened to scale up the business of the FPOs for its long-term growth and viability.

The following challenges need proper attention to provide enabling ecosystem for the FPOs to function:

3.2 Business Plan and Scaling Opportunities

A well-defined business plan is an essential element for the success of any business organization. It becomes more imminent when all the executive members are farmers, who are mostly unskilled about different aspects of any business. The business plan helps the FPOs to diversify and scale up their business activities in a well-planned manner. Currently, majority of the FPOs lack such business plan, and therefore they limit their activity to merely bulk buying and selling of the inputs and/or farm produce

3.3 Difficulties in Marketing of the Produce

FPOs are being recognized on various platforms for procurement by private companies. Private companies find FPOs as a better source for procurement of vegetables and high value crops which helps them cut down the procurement cost and ensure quality to a greater extent. But the practice is limited to few FPOs. However, for long-term sustainability of the FPOs, there is a need of strong market linkage for the farm produce or its value-added products.

3.4 Ownership and Controls

It has also been observed that many FPOs have been formed by few progressive farmers or rural households. These individuals have good intent to support other smallholder farmers in their locality by collectivizing the operations. However, it becomes difficult for such persons to maintain balance between personal interest and the interest of the farmer-members. They also hesitate in handing over the charge of management to democratically elected person within the FPO. This conflict leads to poor governance structure of the FPOs, and over time other members lose interest in participating in the business of the FPOs.

3.5 Poor Capitalization and Funding Scope

There is a provision of funding support under various government schemes to the FPOs promoted by NABARD and/or SFAC. However, such financial assistance is not available to all the FPOs, particularly outside the ambit of NABARD/SFAC. The average paid-up capital (PUC) of majority of the FPOs are between ₹1.0 to 3.0 lakhs. Due to lack of any collateral assets with the FPOs, financial institutions are hesitant to finance the FPOs, unless the latter is well-capitalized. These FPOs find huge challenge in managing their working capital requirements as well. Running a business organization with such small capital base is a daunting task.

3.6 Problems Faced By Farmers to Get Credit

Agriculture is the backbone of Indian economy and it contributes 17.4% to GDP but its contribution is much higher than the world average of 6.1%. Majority of the population in rural areas depends directly or indirectly on agriculture for their livelihood. The recent technological enhancement in agriculture sector which was incepted by green revolution has not resulted in increasing productivity and output, but brought about a significant change in the structure and magnitude in the production process. But the new technology is capital intensive, which is not affordable to small and marginal farmers. The farmers must depend on credit for meeting farm expenses. Therefore, agriculture credit is of prime importance for enhancing production and for removing inequalities.

Agricultural credit is a catalyst that activates other factors of production and plays a crucial role in agricultural market, which is a key element of modernization. It enables farmers to reap economies of scale, venture into new field of production, employ new technologies and empower them to provide utilities for a widening market (AyegbaOjunugwa, 2013). Credit helps farmers to invest in assets in order to generate output and income through deploying science, technology and modern methods of business management (Amit Patel, 2014). Investment in farm can generate farm income substantially. Credit continues to be a developing strategy for the agricultural sector in India. There is a strong demand for agricultural credit and its tremendous contribution to agricultural sector by farmers.

Financial institutions frequently demand collateral inorder to reduce the risk of default, thereby limiting the entry of farmers. On the other hand, it is also the rules, regulation and lending procedures of the financial institutions that create the gap between the farmers, informal lenders are seem to have advantages in terms of lower transaction cost in reaching farmers and therefore, informal continue to remain as a complementary source of credit market in India. (TempaGyeltshen,2012) The problems of the farmers focus attention on adequate supply of credit for improving agricultural activities. The loans processed by financial institutions should fulfil the purpose of borrowing and delay in sanctioning the loans hampers the cultivation. Agricultural credit is available to large farmers and in higher amount, still there are persisting problems in the access of credit. Farmers incur huge transaction costs in obtaining loans due to the cost incurred in frequent visits to the bank, time spent, documentation requirement for availing loans and huge interest costs in small loans.

3.7 General Problems Faced By Farmers

3.7.1 Unavailability of Good Quality of Seeds

Seeds are the basic input or raw material for the farmers to grow crops. But there is a lack of availability of the good quality of seeds in the market. And if the good quality seeds are available, they are so expensive that the poor and marginal farmers are not able to afford.

Due to this, farmers are bound to use the traditional seeds which less productive and yields fewer crops. Most of the certified seeds manufacturers in India are private companies. The government should either tie-up with these companies or provide direct subsidies to the farmers so that they can afford the best quality of seeds for production.

3.7.2 Lack of Modern Equipment

Even in 2020, the majority of Indian farmers use traditional tools for agriculture such as plough, sickle, etc. This leads to the wastage of energy and manpower and less yield per capita labour force. Only little use of the machine is seen in irrigation, harvesting and transportation. There are two reasons why farmers are not using modern equipment. First, they are not aware, and second, they can't afford such equipment. The second problem is, even if a farmer can afford the equipment but there is the unavailability of electricity 24*7 in the village areas.

There is an urgent need to modernize the agricultural operations of the country. Many state governments have started a scheme from which farmers can take modern equipment for rent at a low price. This way they don't have to pay the full sum of amount and they will also get the machines. This is just the start of mechanizing agriculture in India. In recent years there was a huge increase in sales of tractors, power tillers, etc. But India cannot achieve its full agricultural productivity until the whole agriculture system is mechanized.

3.7.3 Poor Irrigation Facilities

Irrigation is one of the essential steps for a crop to grow perfectly. But do you know that only one-third area of the total land in India has proper irrigation facility available? India has the second-largest irrigated land in the world, but still, India faces this problem. Punjab has the highest percentage area of irrigated land in the country of about 98% irrigated land availability, followed by Haryana. The reason for good irrigation facilities is the availability of water throughout the year from the rivers and dam. This helps the farmers to conduct agricultural operations timely.

But scenario all over the country is not the same. In central India, rivers don't carry water throughout the year. Due to this, farmers have to depend on the monsoon water for irrigation which is very uncertain.

3.7.4 Small and Fragmented Holdings of Land

This is one of the major reasons why Indian farmers are not competent. Because, most of the poor farmers have a very small amount of land and that too in a fragmented manner. And according to data, the average size of holding of land per farmers is decreasing every year. It means the situation is getting even worse. This problem becomes more serious in densely populated states with less farming land. Only 1.6% of total land holdings belong to the category of large holding that too by the rich farmers.

It becomes difficult for a farmer to irrigate and harvest in fragmented lands because a lot of time is wasted in moving the resources from one field to another. The main reason for this kind of system is the inheritance law of India. When a person dies, the land belonging to him is distributed among his sons, but this distribution does not insure entailment of a consolidated land. And due to this, most of the farmers in India have fragmented lands.

3.7.5 Dealing with Local Traders and Middleman

It is a problem a farmer faces at the end of all agricultural activity. This is why we have also mentioned it in the end. But don't judge the importance of this problem by its position.

We often see in the news that farmers thrown their crops on roads just because no one purchased it. Due to the absence of mandi houses and proper market places, farmers are not able to sell their crops and get a reasonable price. In this situation, they have to look for a middleman and local traders for business. These middlemen don't provide a reasonable price for their crops, and hence farmers are bound to either sell crops at a lower price or just throw at the roads.

3.7.6 Lack of Storage Facilities

In the absence of a market place, the local traders dominate the market and exploitation of farmers takes place. These middlemen are not only creating a problem for farmers but also for consumers because they ultimately sell the crops at a very high price after purchasing it from farmers. The situation of poor farmers is even worse. They are forced to sell their crops at whatever price is offered to them. Going through these entire problems, how can we expect from our farmers to produce good crops. Instead, we should ask our government to provide the facilities that they deserve.

4

Case Study - Easykrishi

Easykrishi is a young enterprise that uses digital interventions with an aim to change agricultural practices from Reactive Mode to Proactive Mode. It is a consortium of 12 FPOs and 150 Ground Organizations. 14 In a world of declining land-holdings, we realize aggregation of agricultural resources is the only way to keep this planet sustainable for human survival. Aggregation ensures viability and profitability of Agriculture. Easykrishi's baby steps in the entire cycle of aggregation of agricultural resources have made significant impact for Food Producer Corporations across Karnataka and they have made a mark on organizations and individuals that are dedicated for the betterment of Agriculture and farmers.

Easykrishi works towards being the India's largest FPO aggregating platform. It aims at passing on the benefits to the farmers & partner FPOs. Easykrishi aims to bridge the agriculture information gap so that farmers can transact on distant markets, buyers can have predictability in supply chain and agriculture financing institutes can have lower operation cost with pre-qualified lending options.

The Easykrishi app is easy to use and enables real time monitoring of farmer group's activities. The mobile application will be run by a farmer leader who usually handles group 300-1000 farmers. The group can use the mobile application to collect farmer orders (seeds / agricultural inputs) and place a collective order (Demand Aggregation). Production data is entered twice in a season by the village youth who has operational knowledge of internet enabled Smartphone (Supply Aggregation). Supply (agricultural production) information related to:

1. Product Variant (Paddy-M5, Pomegranate-Kesari etc.)
2. Expected Quantity
3. Expected Harvest Date
4. Expected Price

This application helps the relevant agencies keep track of all activities in real time and even works offline and has language option.

4.1 Benefits of the Easykrishi Application Farmer Group

The mobile application helps the

Farmer leader

1. Collect all the member orders and collectively buy the agricultural inputs
2. Real time production information helps the leader schedule the delivery to the bulk customers
3. Monitor the ground activities on mobile and help farmers with agricultural advisories (pesticide/fertilizer application scheduling)
4. Agricultural Financing Institutions: The mobile application helps the Financing Institutions
5. To monitor ground activities of farmer in real time
6. To predict the agricultural production and plan for post-harvest activities (warehouse receipt financing)
7. To reduce NPAs by having farmer level information
8. To build better and newer products for farmers in ever changing agricultural scenario
9. Policy Makers and Advisory Bodies: The mobile application helps the policy Makers and Advisory bodies
10. Creates a massive digital network for cost effective communication at the farmer level
11. Helps monitor the effectiveness of the programs in real time
12. Helps estimate the right amount of support required down at the farm level
13. Helps manage the ground assets and monitor its use in real time

4.2 Group Purchasing

Easykrishi has facilitated the meeting between the input selling companies and the farmer producing companies and helped both of them trade at a competitive price. Group Selling EasyKrishi had organized a successful Buyer Sellers Meet in March 2018. The Buyers included Aditya Birla's More, Spar Hypermart, BigBasket and many more. The Buyers were very much interested in knowing which Farmers producer company had which product and at what quantity. This was the most important information buyers obtained from the meet. The trading happened on a good note and the farmer producer companies were able to obtain a good price for their produce and sell huge quantities of their produce. On the similar lines Hotels Connect was also organized and business worth one and half lakh took place.

5

Information Technology (IT) for Agriculture

5.1 Robotics in Agriculture

Since the industrial revolution in the 1800s, automation got more advanced to efficiently handle sophisticated tasks and increase production. With increasing demands and shortage of labor across the globe, agriculture robots or commonly known as Agribots are starting to gain attention among farmers. Crop production decreased by an estimated 213 crores approx ($3.1 billion) a year due to labor shortages in the USA alone. Recent advancements in sensors and AI technology that lets machines train on their surroundings have made agrobots more notable. We are still in the early stages of an ag-robotics revolution, harnessing the full potential of the Internet of Things in agriculture, with most of the products still in early trial phases and R&D mode.

Fig.5.1: Weeding Robots

These smart Agri robots use digital image processing to look through the images of weeds in their database to detect similarities with crops and weed out or spray them directly with their robotic arms. With an increasing number of plants becoming resistant to pesticides they are a boon to the environment and also to farmers who used to spread the pesticides throughout the farm. An estimated 13,000 kilograms (3 billion pounds) of herbicides are applied at a cost of 1,725 crores ($25B) each year, thus reducing their overall cost.

Fig. 5.2: Machine Navigation

As remote-controlled toy cars are enabled with a controller, tractors and heavy plowing equipment can be run automatically from the comfort of home through GPS. These integrated automatic machines are highly accurate and self-adjust when they detect differences in terrains, simplifying labor-intensive tasks. Their movements as well as work progress can be easily checked on smartphones. With advancements in IoT in Agricultural and machine learning, these tech-driven motors are enabling Advanced farming using IoT independently with features such as automatic obstacle detection.

Fig. 5.3: Harvesting Robotics

Utilizing agribots to pick crops is solving the problem of labor shortages. Working the delicate process of picking fruits and vegetables these innovative machines can operate 24/7. A combination of image processing and robotic arms is used by these machines to determine the fruits to pick hence controlling the quality. Due to high operational costs, crops that have an early focus on agribot harvesting are orchard fruits like apples. Greenhouse harvesting also finds applications with these bots for high-value crops like tomatoes and strawberries. These bots can work in greenhouses to aptly determine the stage of crops and harvest them at the right time.

Fig. 4.4: Material Handling

Robots can perform dreaded manual labor tasks working alongside the labors. They can lift heavy materials and perform tasks like plant spacing with high accuracy, therefore optimizing the space and plant quality and reducing production costs.

5.2. Drones in Agriculture

Drones in agriculture are used to enhance and optimize various farming activities such as crop monitoring, crop spraying, soil analysis, and mapping. In fact, agriculture is one of the major sectors to incorporate drones. Drones equipped with sensors and cameras are used for imaging, mapping, and surveying farms. There are ground-based drones and aerial drones. Ground drones are bots that survey the fields on wheels. Aerial drones, formally known as unmanned aerial vehicles (UAVs) or unmanned aircraft systems (UAS), are flying robots. Drones can be controlled remotely or they can fly automatically through software-controlled flight plans in their embedded systems, working in coordination with sensors and GPS. From the drone data, insights can be drawn regarding crop health, irrigation, spraying, planting, soil and field, plant counting, yield prediction, and much more. Drones can either be scheduled for farm surveys (drone as a service) or can be bought and stored near farms where they can be recharged and maintained. After the surveys, the drones need to be taken to nearby labs to analyze the data that has been collected, thereby helping leverage IoT in agriculture better.

Fig. 5.5: Drone Handling

5.3. Remote Sensing in Agriculture

Remote sensing in agriculture is revolutionizing the way data is acquired from different nodes in a farm' IoT-based remote sensing utilizes sensors placed along with the farms like weather stations for gathering data, which is transmitted to analytical tools for analysis. Sensors are devices sensitive to anomalies. Farmers can monitor the crops from the analytical dashboard and take action based on insights.

Fig. 5.6 : Crops Monitoring

1. Crop Monitoring: Sensors placed along the farms monitor the crops for changes in light, humidity, temperature, shape, and size. Any anomaly detected by the sensors is analyzed and the farmer is notified. Thus remote sensing can help prevent the spread of diseases and keep an eye on the growth of crops.
2. Weather conditions: The data collected by sensors in terms of humidity, temperature, moisture precipitation, and dew detection helps in determining the weather pattern in farms so that cultivation is done for suitable crops.
3. Soil quality: Soil health analysis helps in determining the nutrient value and drier areas of farms, soil drainage capacity, or acidity, which allows for adjustment of the amount of water needed for irrigation and opting for

the most beneficial type of cultivation. The soil health data can also help leverage regenerative agriculture by providing insights into how and when to increase organic matter and therefore achieve a better soil structure and eventually pave a path for climate-smart agriculture.

5.4. Computer Imaging In Agriculture

Computer imaging involves the use of sensor cameras installed at different corners of the farm or drones equipped with cameras to produce images that undergo digital image processing. Digital image processing is the basic concept of processing an input image using computer algorithms. Image processing views the images in different spectral intensities such as infrared, compares the images obtained over a period of time, and detects anomalies, thus analyzing limiting factors and helping a better management of farms.

Fig. 5.7: Crops Monitoring

Quality control

Image processing combined with machine learning uses images from database to compare with images of crops to determine the size, shape, color and growth therefore controlling the quality.

Sorting and grading

Post harvest, computer imaging can increase accuracy and time-efficiency of sorting and grading agricultural and food products based on their size, texture, color and shape.

Irrigation Monitoring

Irrigation monitoring over a period of time helps in mapping irrigated lands. It also enables optimum irrigation scheduling based on soil moisture conditions, varying weather patterns, and plant physiological conditions.

5.5 Smart Agriculture System Using IOT: In Simple Words

IoT device includes every object that can be controlled through the Internet. IoT devices have become commonplace in consumer markets with wearable IoWT (Internet of Wearable Things), such as smartwatches, and home management products, like Google home. It is estimated over 30 billion devices could be connected to the Internet of Things by 2020. The applications of the Internet of Things in agriculture target conventional farming operations to meet the increasing demands and decrease production losses. IoT in agriculture uses robots, drones, remote sensors, and computer imaging combined with continuously progressing machine learning and analytical tools for monitoring crops, surveying, and mapping the fields, and providing data to farmers for rational farm management plans to save both time and money.

Till now the Industrial Internet of Things (IoT) has disrupted many industries and the Agriculture Industry isn't an exception. Till the end of 2018, the connected agriculture market stood at USD 1.8 billion globally and the change hasn't stopped yet. It is expected to grow to USD 4.3 billion by 2023 at a Compound Annual Growth Rate (CAGR) of 19.3%. The IoT technology has realized the smart wearable's, connected devices, automated machines, and driverless cars. However, in agriculture, the IoT has brought the greatest impact.

Recent statistics reveal that the global population is about to reach 9.6 billion by 2050. And to feed this massive population, the agriculture industry is bounded to adopt the Internet of Things. Amongst the challenges like extreme weather conditions, climatic changes, environmental impact, IoT is eradicating these challenges and helping us to meet the demand for more food. Throughout the world, mechanical innovations such as tractors and harvesters took place and brought into the agriculture operations in the late 20th century. And the agriculture Industry relies heavily on innovative ideas because of the steadily growing demand for food.

The Industrial IoT has been a driving force behind increased agricultural production at a lower cost. In the next several years, the use of smart solutions powered by IoT will increase in the agriculture operations. In fact, few of the recent report tells that the IoT device installation will see a compound annual growth rate of 20% in the agriculture industry. And the no. of connected devices (agricultural) will grow from 13 million in 2014 to 225 million by 2024. Due to lack of constant and reliable communication network infrastructure, an IoT solutions provider as well as the business owners had faced implementation challenges in remote or less developed regions. But, many network providers are making it possible by introducing satellite connectivity and expending cellular networks.

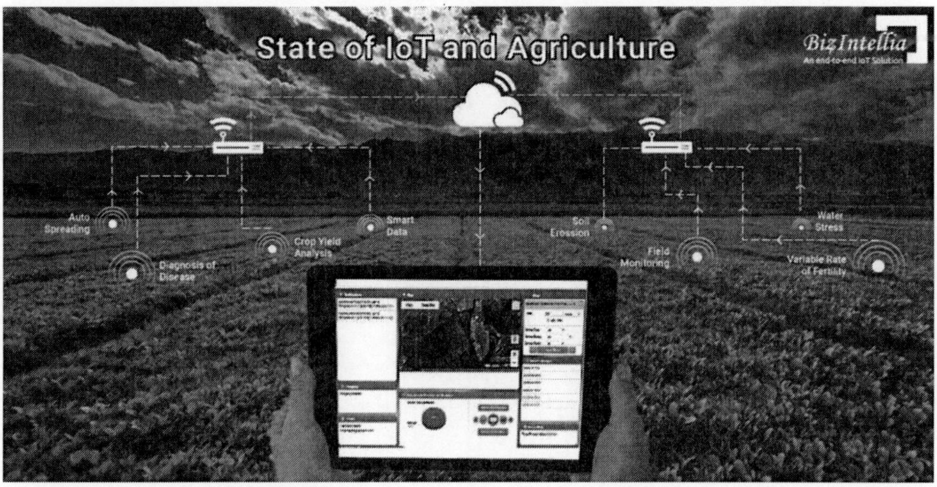

Fig. 5.8: How IoT in Agriculture took its footprints?

It's been long since sensors were introduced in the agriculture operations. But the problem with the traditional approach of utilizing sensor technology was that we were not able to get the live data from the sensors. The sensors used to log the data into their attached memory and later on we were able to use it. With the introduction of Industrial IoT in Agriculture, far more advanced sensors are being utilized. The sensors are now connected to the cloud via cellular/satellite network. Which lets us to know the real-time data from the sensors, making decision making effective.

The applications of IoT in the agriculture industry has helped the farmers to monitor the water tank levels in real-time which makes the irrigation process more efficient. The advancement of IoT technology in agriculture operations has brought the use of sensors in every step of the farming process like how much time and resources a seed takes to become a fully-grown vegetable. Internet of Things in Agriculture has come up as a second wave of green revolution. The benefits that the farmers are getting by adapting IoT are twofold. It has helped farmers to decrease their costs and increase yields at the same time by improving farmer's decision making with accurate data.

6

Applicability of IoT in Agriculture

Smart Farming is a hi-tech and effective system of doing agriculture and growing food in a sustainable way. It is an application of implementing connected devices and innovative technologies together into agriculture. Smart Farming majorly depends on IoT thus eliminating the need of physical work of farmers and growers and thus increasing the productivity in every possible manner.

With the recent agriculture trends dependent on agriculture, Internet of Things has brought huge benefits like efficient use of water, optimization of inputs and many more. What made difference were the huge benefits and which has become a revolutionized agriculture in the recent days. IoT based Smart Farming improves the entire Agriculture system by monitoring the field in real-time. With the help of sensors and interconnectivity, the Internet of Things in Agriculture has not only saved the time of the farmers but has also reduced the extravagant use of resources such as Water and Electricity. It keeps various factors like humidity, temperature, soil etc. under check and gives a crystal clear real-time observation.

The following are the benefits of adopting new technology - Internet of Things in Agriculture:

1. Climate Conditions

Fig. 6.1: How IoT in Agriculture - Climate

Climate plays a very critical role for farming. And having improper knowledge about climate heavily deteriorates the quantity and quality of the crop production. But IoT solutions enable you to know the real-time weather conditions. Sensors are placed inside and outside of the agriculture fields. They collect data from the environment which is used to choose the right crops which can grow and sustain in the particular climatic conditions. The whole IoT ecosystem is made up of sensors that can detect real-time weather conditions like humidity, rainfall, temperature and more very accurately.

There are numerous no. of sensors available to detect all these parameters and configure accordingly to suit your smart farming requirements. These sensors monitor the condition of the crops and the weather surrounding them. If any disturbing weather conditions are found, then an alert is send. What gets eliminated is the need of the physical presence during disturbing climatic conditions which eventually increases the productivity and help farmers to reap more agriculture benefits.

6.1. Precision Farming

Fig. 6.2: Precision Farming

Precision Agriculture/Precision Farming is one of the most famous applications of IoT in Agriculture. It makes the farming practice more precise and controlled by realizing smart farming applications such as livestock monitoring, vehicle tracking, field observation, and inventory monitoring. The goal of precision farming is to analyze the data, generated via sensors, to react accordingly. Precision Farming helps farmers to generate data with the help of sensors and analyze that information to take intelligent and quick decisions.

There are numerous precision farming techniques like irrigation management, livestock management, vehicle tracking and many more which play a vital role in increasing the efficiency and effectiveness. With the help of Precision farming, you can analyze soil conditions and other related parameters to increase the operational efficiency. Not only this you can also detect the real-time working conditions of the connected devices to detect water and nutrient level.

6.2 Smart Greenhouse

Fig. 6.3: Smart Greenhouse

To make our greenhouses smart, IoT has enabled weather stations to automatically adjust the climate conditions according to a particular set of instructions. Adoption of IoT in Greenhouses has eliminated the human intervention, thus making entire process cost-effective and increasing accuracy at the same time. For example, using solar-powered IoT sensors builds modern and inexpensive greenhouses.

These sensors collect and transmit the real-time data which helps in monitoring the greenhouse state very precisely in real-time. With the help of the sensors, the water consumption and greenhouse state can be monitored via emails or SMS alerts. Automatic and smart irrigation is carried out with the help of IoT. These sensors help to provide information on the pressure, humidity, temperature and light levels.

6.3 Data Analytics

The conventional database system does not have enough storage for the data collected from the IoT sensors. Cloud based data storage and an end-to-end IoT Platform plays an important role in the smart agriculture system. These systems are estimated to play an important role such that better activities can be performed. In the IoT world, sensors are the primary source of collecting data on a large scale. The data is analyzed and transformed to meaningful information using analytics tools. The data analytics helps in the analysis of weather conditions, livestock conditions, and crop conditions.

Fig. 6.4: Data Analytics

The data collected leverages the technological innovations and thus making better decisions. With the help of the IoT devices, you can know the real-time status of the crops by capturing the data from sensors. Using predictive analytics, you can get an insight to make better decisions related to harvesting. The trend analysis helps the farmers to know upcoming weather conditions and harvesting of crops. IoT in the Agriculture Industry has helped the farmers to maintain the quality of crops and fertility of the land, thus enhancing the product volume and quality.

6.4. Agricultural Drones

Fig. 6.5: Agricultural Drones

Technological advancements has almost revolutionized the agricultural operations and the introduction of agricultural drones is the trending disruption.

The Ground and Aerial drones are used for assessment of crop health, crop monitoring, planting, crop spraying, and field analysis. With proper strategy and planning based on real-time data, drone technology has given a high rise and makeover to the agriculture industry. Drones with thermal or multispectral sensors identify the areas that require changes in irrigation. Once the crops start growing, sensors indicate their health and calculate their vegetation index. Eventually smart drones have reduced the environmental impact. The results have been such that there has been a massive reduction and much lower chemical reaching the groundwater.

IoT enabled agriculture has helped implement modern technological solutions to time tested knowledge. This has helped bridge the gap between production and quality and quantity yield. Data Ingested by obtaining and importing information from the multiple sensors for real time use or storage in a database ensures swift action and less damage to the crops. With seamless end to end intelligent operations and improved business process execution, produce gets processed faster and reaches supermarkets in fastest time possible.

Fig. 6.6 : Smart Farming/Agriculture

6.5 Hardware Used

Intellia INT G01- Soil Moisture Sensor

Intellia INT G01- Soil Moisture Sensor (Transmitter) is a high precision, high sensitivity soil moisture measuring instrument. This product is a metal shell, high compressive strength, good sealing performance; the use of electromagnetic pulse principle to measure the apparent dielectric constant of the soil.

Quick Specifications

Model No	INT G01
Monitoring principle	FDR
Structure	4-pintype
Output Signal	4-20mA
PowerSupply	DC12-24V
Response time	< 1s

6.6 Intellia Soil PH Sensor INT-PH1

The transmitter is widely used in soil PH detection, sewage treatment and other occasions requiring PH monitoring. The three parts of input power, induction probe and signal output are completely isolated. It's safe and reliable and with beautiful appearance, easy to be installed.

Quick Specifications

Model No	INT-PH1
Power consumption	≤0.15W (@12V DC , 25°C)
Measuring accuracy	±0.5pH
Measuring range	0-14pH
Operating temperature	0-65°C
Output signal	RS485 (Modbus protocol)

IOT is an acronym for Internet of Things. It means accessing and controlling daily usable devices and equipments using the Internet. The term "Things" in the Internet of Things refers to anything and everything in day-to-day life which is accessed or connected through the internet. IOT is an advanced automation and analytics system that deals with artificial intelligence, sensor, networking, electronic, cloud messaging, etc., to deliver complete systems for the product or services.

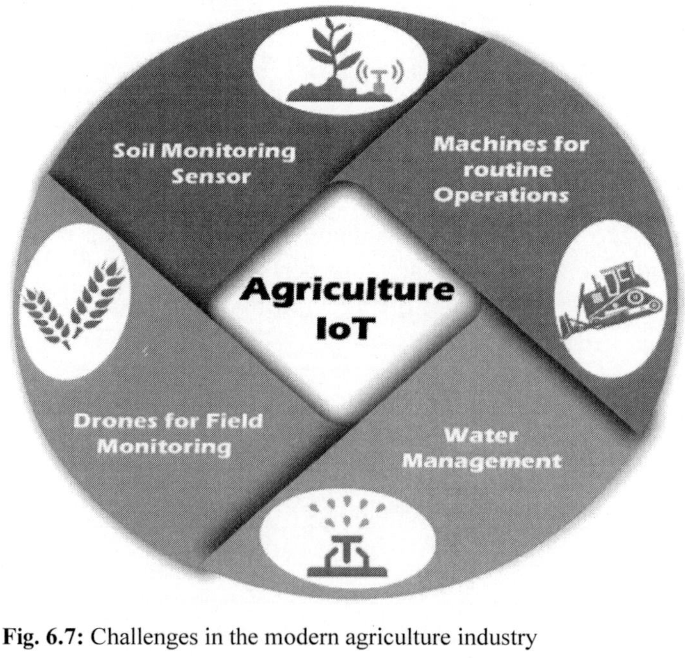

Fig. 6.7: Challenges in the modern agriculture industry

By the year 2050, the world's growing population is estimated to have reached about 10 billion. To feed such a large population, agriculture needs to marry technology and get the best results. Agriculture is another important domain for IOT. IOT systems play an important role for crop and soil monitoring and give a proper solution accordingly. IOT leads to smart farming. Using IOT, farmers can minimize waste and increase productivity. The system allows the monitoring of fields with the help of sensors. Farmers can monitor the status of the area.

The challenges faced by the farming industry and agriculture are listed as follows :

1. Lack of workforce and manpower
2. Environmental challenges and global warming
3. Requirement of large manual intervention
4. Lack of proper monitoring
5. Challenges in analyzing the large scale unstructured data

There are various uses of IOT in agriculture that are discussed as follows -

6.7 What Is a Smart Farm?

Smart farming refers to managing farms using modern Information and communication technologies to increase the quantity and quality of products while optimizing the human labor required.

Among the technologies available for present-day farmers are:

1. **Sensors**: Soil, water, light, humidity, temperature management
2. **Software**: Specialized software solutions that target specific farm types or applications agnostic IoT platforms
3. **Connectivity**: Cellular, LoRa
4. **Location**: GPS, Satellite
5. **Robotics**: Autonomous tractors, processing facilities
6. **Data analytics**: Standalone analytics solutions, data pipelines for downstream solutions

Armed with such tools, farmers can monitor field conditions and make strategic decisions for the whole farm or a single plant without even needing to step foot in the field.

The driving force of smart farming is IoT— connecting machines and sensors integrated on farms to make farming processes data-driven and automated.

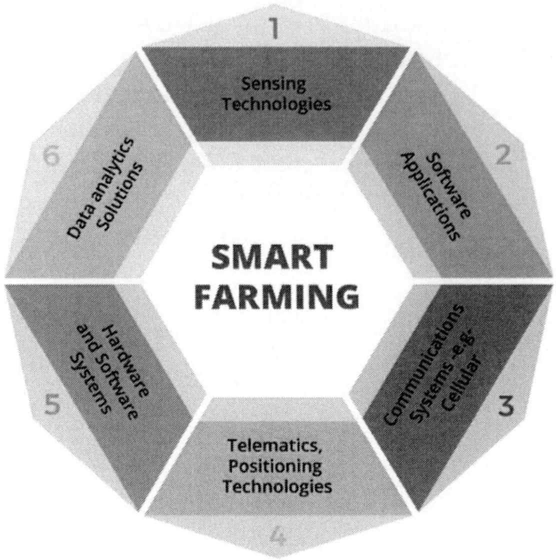

Fig. 6.8: Smart Farming

6.8 The IoT-Based Smart Farming Cycle

The core of IoT is the data you can draw from things and transmit over the internet. To optimize the farming process, IoT devices installed on a farm should collect and process data in a repetitive cycle that enables farmers to react quickly to emerging issues and changes in ambient conditions. Smart farming follows a cycle similar to this one:

1. **Observation**. Sensors record observational data from the crops, livestock, soil, or atmosphere.
2. **Diagnostics.** The sensor values are fed to a cloud-hosted IoT platform with predefined decision rules and models—also called "business logic"—that ascertain the condition of the examined object and identify any deficiencies or needs.
3. **Decisions**. After issues are revealed, the user, and/or machine learning-driven components of the IoT platform determine whether location-specific treatment is necessary and, if so, which.
4. **Action**. After end-user evaluation and action, the cycle repeats from the beginning.

6.9 IoT Solutions to Agricultural Problems

Many believe that IoT can add value to all areas of farming, from growing crops to forestry. While there are several ways that IoT can improve farming, two of the major ways IoT can revolutionize agriculture are precision farming and farming automation.

Precision Farming

Precision farming, or precision agriculture, is an umbrella concept for IoT-based approaches that make farming more controlled and accurate. In simple words, plants and cattle get precisely the treatment they need, determined by machines with superhuman accuracy. The biggest difference from the classical approach is that precision farming allows decisions to be made per square meter or even per plant/animal rather than for a field.

By precisely measuring variations within a field, farmers can boost the effectiveness of pesticides and fertilizers, or use them selectively.

Precision Livestock Farming

As is the case of precision agriculture, smart farming techniques enable farmers better to monitor the needs of individual animals and adjust their nutrition accordingly, thereby preventing disease and enhancing herd health.

Large farm owners can use wireless IoT applications to monitor the location, well-being, and health of their cattle. With this information, they can identify sick animals, so that they can be separated from the herd to prevent the spread of disease.

Automation in Smart Greenhouses

Traditional greenhouses control the environmental parameters through manual intervention or a proportional control mechanism, which often results in production loss, energy loss, and increased labor costs.

IoT-driven smart greenhouses can intelligently monitor as well as control the climate, eliminating the need for manual intervention. Various sensors are deployed to measure the environmental parameters according to the specific requirements of the crop. That data is stored in a cloud-based platform for further processing and control with minimal manual intervention.

6.10 Third Green Revolution

Smart farming and IoT-driven agriculture are paving the way for what can be called a Third Green Revolution. Following the plant breeding and genetics revolutions, the Third Green Revolution is taking over agriculture. That revolution draws upon the combined application of data-driven analytics technologies, such as precision farming equipment, IoT, big data analytics, Unmanned Aerial Vehicles (UAVs or drones), robotics, etc.

In the future, this smart farming revolution depicts, pesticide and fertilizer use will drop while overall efficiency will rise. IoT technologies will enable better food traceability, which in turn will lead to increased food safety. It will also be beneficial for the environment, through, for example, more efficient use of water, or optimization of treatments and inputs.

Therefore, smart farming has a real potential to deliver a more productive and sustainable form of agricultural production, based on a more precise and resource-efficient approach. New farms will finally realize the eternal dream of mankind. It'll feed our population, which may explode to 9.8 billion by 2050.

Smart Farming for Food Safety

The Global Farming industry is facing many food safety challenges like non-standardized pest control, varying weather conditions, and also unpredictable contamination. These challenges are the sources of many diseases that cause great harm to human health. It also could negatively impact the credibility of food producers and manufacturers while exporting food products.

As the food supply chain is getting more and more complex, along with tough local and international food safety regulations, SaaS-based smart farming solutions, can transform the way the entire Agri supply chain is managed.

Such solutions bring observability to agribusinesses, and help them predict any anomalies and take corrective actions to prevent any food safety issue, in a cost-effective way.

What is Smart Farming?

Smart farming centers on growing farm productivity using technology - hardware and software. Smart farming focuses on managing farms, plantations, and all associated farming activities using IoT, drones, robotics, machinery, and artificial intelligence, to determine a path to predictable farm output.

Smart Farming is focused on the use of data acquired through various sources (historical, geographical, and instrumental) in the management of farm activities. Technologically advanced doesn't essentially mean that it is a smart system. Smart agriculture technologies differentiate themselves through their ability to record the data and make sense of it. Smart farming employs hardware (IoT) and software (Software as a Service or SaaS) to capture the data and give actionable insights to manage all the operations on the farm, both pre-and post-harvest. The data is organized, accessible all the time, and full of data on every aspect of finance and field operations that can be monitored from anywhere in the world.

Differences between Traditional and Smart Farming

Implementing robotics in agriculture and other smart farming techniques brings in several benefits over conventional farming strategies. Some of these include exercising increased control over production processes, which in turn enhances cost management and reduces waste generation. In addition to this, smart farming, through the implementation of new technology in agriculture, makes it easier to trace anomalies in crop growth as well as livestock health.

6.11 Smart Farming Technologies Including IoT

IoT in agriculture involves sensors, drones, and robots connected through the internet which function automatically and semi-automatically performing operations and gathering data aimed at increasing efficiency and predictability. With increasing demands and shortage of labor across the globe, agriculture automation and robots or commonly known as agribots are starting to gain attention among farmers. Crop production decreased by an estimated 213 crores approx ($3.1 billion) a year due to labor shortages in the USA alone. Recent advancements in sensors and AI technology that lets machines train on their surroundings have made agri-bots more notable.

John Deere, the 200-year-old American farm equipment company is already connecting its ubiquitous tractors to the internet. Farmers now know their tractor productivity on their phones. John Deere extended this to help display crop yields on farmers' smartphones. Thanks to Tesla, the smart car bug has hit tractors too. John Deere is in the works to develop self-driving tractors, which would not just free up farmers' time but also improve farm safety.

The world is in the early stages of an ag-robotics revolution with most of the products still in R&D and trial phases.

Smart Greenhouses

Smart greenhouses are revolutionizing the agricultural industry by creating a self-sustaining microclimate perfect for crop production. Controlled environments allow farmers to eliminate worries of unpredictable weather or predators while harvesting real-time data that maximizes efficiency and improves yields with precision irrigation, temperature control, lighting adjustment, and more.

Semi-Automatic Robots

Semi-automatic robots with arms can detect weeds and spray pesticides on the affected plants, preventing extensive damage as well as reducing the overall pesticide costs. These robots can also be used in harvesting and lifting. Heavy farming vehicles can also be navigated from the comfort of homes through phone screens to perform tasks and GPS can track their positions at any time.

Drones

Drones in agriculture are equipped with sensors and cameras and are used for imaging, mapping, and surveying farms. They can be remotely controlled or they can fly automatically through agriculture software-controlled flight plans in their embedded systems, working in coordination with sensors and GPS. From the drone data, insights can be drawn regarding crop health, irrigation, spraying, planting, soil and field, plant counting and yield prediction, and much more.

Smart Remote Sensing

Remote sensing utilizes sensors like weather stations placed on farms to gather data, which is then transmitted to analytical tools for analysis. They monitor the crops for changes in light, humidity, temperature, shape, and size. The data collected by sensors in terms of humidity, temperature, moisture precipitation, and dew detection helps in determining the weather pattern in farms so that cultivation is done for suitable crops. The analysis of the soil quality helps in determining the nutrient value and drier areas of farms, soil drainage capacity, or acidity, which allows for adjusting the amount of water needed for irrigation and the opt most beneficial type of cultivation.

Computer imaging

Computer imaging involves the use of sensor cameras installed at different points on the farm or drones equipped with cameras. The images they capture undergo digital processing to derive meaningful insights from them. They are used for quality control, disease detection, irrigation monitoring, and sorting and grading the produce after harvest. Image processing using machine learning incorporates comparing images from a database with images of standing crops to determine the size, shape, color, and growth, therefore controlling the quality.

7

Smart Farming with Saas-Based Cloud Software

Cloud-based software is used for the management of financial and field activities of farms. Prior to computers, farmers maintained data manually by keeping lengthy records on papers. This method was prone to human calculation errors. After the computer boom in the 1980s, it was not long before finance software such as Money Counts came to market. They intended to replace the spreadsheets to maintain the financial data.

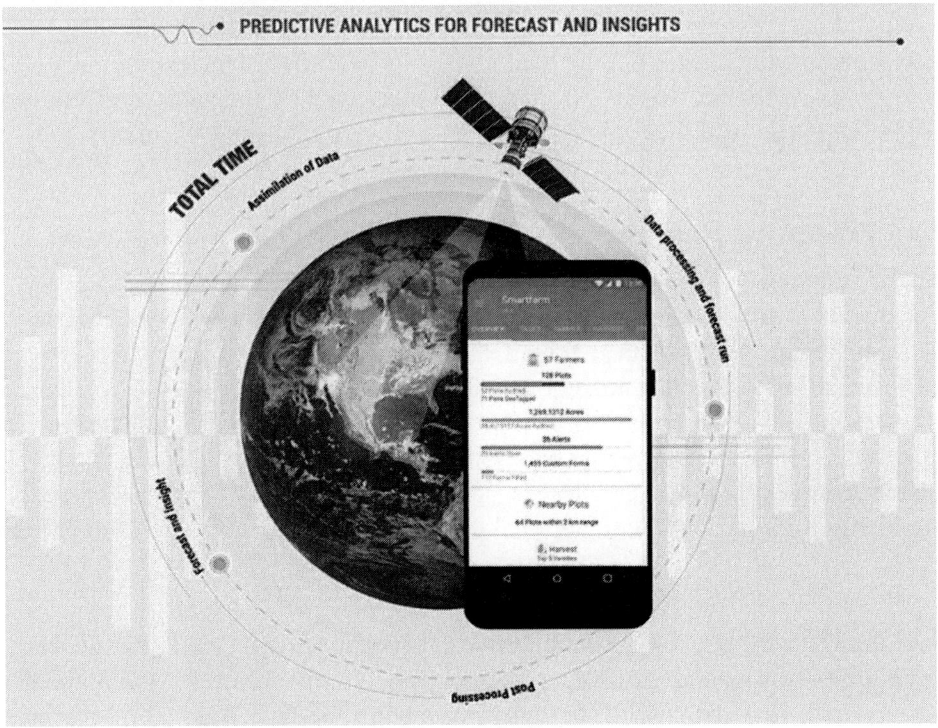

Fig. 7.1 : Smart Farming with Saas-based cloud software

The biggest challenge that farmers faced was the inability to manage field data. To address this, around the mid-2000s, satellite image use with tools like

Raven Receiver for field zone tracking became widely used. Farmers had to implement and coordinate different tools to manage complete farm operations.

With constant improvements through the years, Agri tech SaaS has become an all-in-one tool for the management of all these activities and more in one place using a single tool. This is also enabling the entire smart farming cycle for good. Agritech cloud software has a strong role play too, in each step of the smart farming cycle.

- Collection - Collecting as much data as possible
- Analysis
- Decision
- Action

Data Collection

One of the biggest applications of cloud-based software in agriculture is for data collection and retrieval. It stores high volumes of data relating to weather, crop patterns, soil quality, harvesting, and satellite imagery to provide insights with accuracy and speed. All the data related to the farm is stored in the cloud and hence readily accessible. So, if crops are affected by the same symptoms as 10 years ago, the data can be used to find a remedy more quickly than before, preventing extensive losses.

Data Processing Analysis

Database management in cloud software ties up all the loose ends of every type of data available with respect to farms to enable higher levels of decision-making. Meteorological data, market data, farm data, GIS, and water availability. All forms of historical and current data are analyzed thoroughly before giving valuable insights into optimum seed, water, and pesticide requirements for a farm. The systems also have an alert system whenever discrepancies in crop growth are detected. Hence these systems work efficiently in case of pest attack informing farmers with actionable data.

Data Storage and Dissemination

Data storage is the backbone of predictive analysis. Earlier the data storage was hardware-based, hence the infrastructure needed to be carefully maintained and updated. Any damage to the hardware meant the data was gone forever. Nowadays, agritech systems are cloud-based, which means that one need not invest in purchasing and maintaining hardware. All the data is available all the time and can even be accessed through PCs and mobile gadgets. This approach to data storage also makes it accessible for other devices and solutions to consume it for further analysis. The more the data available relating to farms, the more accurate the insights pertaining to crop production and management, pest and disease detection, crop yield estimation, and others.

7.1 Smart Farming is Trending with Caution

The management consulting firm Mckinsey recently published "Voice of the US farmer in 2022" survey. The survey covered over 1,300 farmers across large, medium, and small farms across the US.

The survey captured farmer responses across many challenges - climate change, geopolitical tension, supply chain issues, inflation, and volatility. The overall sentiment is of caution. Nevertheless, the survey found that farmers are embracing agtech to manage market uncertainty. Agtech adoption has increased in the past 2 years but scaling challenges remain. ROI (return on investment) and poor farmer experience are the main impediments to scaling successfully.

The challenge with scalability was documented well in a similar 2-year-old Mckinsey survey that focused on the value generated by the digital smart farming solution. The survey found that less than 40 percent of respondents self-reported positive returns. The critical success factors were found to be no different than those that mattered in corporate digital transformation initiatives.

1. Leadership commitment
2. Business case alignment
3. At-scale investment

About two-thirds of survey respondents indicated they had just one critical success factor, hinting at a lack of project preparation. Even those with all the success factors in place reported negative results. Yet even some survey respondents with the right ingredients in place still reported negative returns. Perhaps there is more to unravel when making smart farming agtech investments.

At a worldwide level, there is general acceptance that smart farming is the way to go in order to balance the pressure of demand with the need for sustainability.

7.2 Climate Smart Agriculture

Climate smart agriculture (CSA) is an approach to agriculture that aims to help farmers adapt to and mitigate the effects of climate change. CSA focuses on three main pillars: increasing productivity, reducing emissions, and improving resilience. One way to increase productivity is to use climate-resistant crops or varieties. For example, heat-tolerant varieties of rice can be planted in areas that are prone to droughts. Another way to reduce emissions is to improve farm management practices, such as using more efficient irrigation systems. Finally, CSA also involves building resilience into farming systems, such as by diversifying crops and using early warning systems for extreme weather events. By adopting climate smart agriculture practices, farmers can help to keep their operations running smoothly in the face of a changing climate.

7.3 Smart Farming by Cropin

Smart farming focuses on the application of captured data and combining it from various data sources to show the bigger picture to manage all the activities of the farm. Smart farming is a big leap from traditional farming as it brings certainty and predictability to the table which is the Future of Agriculture.

Robotics, drones, and sensors placed throughout the farms can collect data that can be processed to produce farm insights. Cloud-based software can be used to collect the data from farms and combine them with other sources of data to determine yield output, irrigation scheduling, disease outbreaks, pest infestations, and the like. It can also consume off-farm data, such as market information and dealer availability, to enable informed decision-making post-harvest processes.

As a global agritech, Cropin has worked with 200+ public and private sector organizations worldwide, utilizing deep learning, satellite monitoring, cloud computing, precision agriculture, and other technological advancements to collect, analyze data, and manage all the activities from farm to fork with streamlined farm solutions.

Cropin's SaaS solution is beneficial for farming companies, lending and insurance institutions, food processing companies, insurance providers, seed production, non-profit organizations, and government agencies.

Innovative ideas and technologies allow us to improve the efficiency and safety of the food industry. In that sense, IoT's main contribution to that sector is giving it the ability to continuously monitor food throughout its production, processing, transportation, and retailing.

Real-time data gathered by IoT devices makes it possible to closely monitor food safety parameters from "farm to table", thus reducing the risk of foodborne illness outbreaks. Here are some examples of how IoT can boost food safety through enhanced data collection and automated reporting:

- ***At the farm.*** IoT can be used, for example, during crop growth to collect and share data about the soil conditions and the properties of the irrigation water. This can be done through smart sensors built to detect harmful chemical substances and heavy metals that can contaminate the crops.

Furthermore, in food-producing animals, smart sensors can also be used to monitor their health and *manure* to avoid risks of foodborne diseases.

- ***During transportation.*** IoT can significantly improve traceability, allowing all stakeholders to track goods at every point. The connected devices can do more than providing stakeholders with information about the temperature and conditions in which the goods were transported (including if at some point they were exposed to higher or lower temperatures than advised, compromising their safety). They can also help answer crucial questions for decision-making such as: where do the goods come from and which path did they take to arrive here? How long were the goods stored and at what locations? Due to transportation circumstances, are there products that require better (un)loading or more efficient sorting? All, without the need for time-consuming, imprecise, and costly manual data collection.
- ***In supermarkets.*** Shelves can be made "smart" with IoT to measure the freshness of the products as well as their storage period and conditions (e.g., humidity, temperature, and pressure). Furthermore, by measuring the evolution of early warning parameters of perishables such as quantity of pathogen agents, gases, weight changes and PH, actions can be taken to reduce the shelf-life of the product and to get it to a consumer's plate before it goes bad.
- ***In restaurants.*** IoT technology can detect traces of harmful pathogens, and hence tell food handlers when their hands are not properly washed (hands are a common vehicle for the transfer of dangerous microorganisms to food). Furthermore, food is also at risk of hazards when in refrigeration equipment and food cooking or warming equipment. To avoid the risks, food service operators are required to manually record temperature at regular intervals and keep the logs for periodic inspections. This practice has several limitations which IoT can easily address, including: minimal data sampling; rushed and inaccurate data collection; and inaccessible records (illegible, damaged, or lost). Additionally, IoT empowered kitchen appliances can regulate storage and inventory levels, conduct analyses, and thus prevent food waste by providing precise actionable insight on ingredient demand.

7.4 IoT: The key Ingredient for Food Safety

Achieving effective food safety systems is a shared responsibility that requires all stakeholders across the chain to collaborate and work together. It is a serious matter, and it is everyone's business. However, it can be more complicated than it seems without a data-backed process that provides real-time knowledge to make better decisions.

IoT technology is the natural ally to increase our ability to prevent, detect and respond to the health threats associated with unsafe food. Due to their flexible nature, IoT solutions can be applied in countless ways to help the food industry. In that sense, many solutions are waiting to be embraced and applied before we can see the desired and needed results in food safety.

According to the National Resources Defense Council (NRDC), approx. 40 % food worth $165 billion get wasted yearly. In fact, we could have provided a 2,000-calorie diet to the 84% of the American population if we were able to recover the wasted food. It is a painful fact that most of the food wastage happens after harvesting pointing the blame towards inefficient Food Supply Chain.

IoT (Internet of Things) is already putting a major dent to this and has the potential to solve world hunger. It's a multidimensional problem and requires a comprehensive IoT solution to crack it. We predict that by end of 2020 the world will be dependent on IoT technology regarding food supply chain and it's safety, the IoT technology will tell us if the food on our plate is safe to consume or not. e-Nose, powered by IoT will be entrusted even more than a human nose.

"Expiry date label on food packaging will be the thing of past."

In most of the cases, the intentions behind throwing the food away are not ill. However, we think that foods are unsafe because they don't appear fresh. We throw away because we are confused about the expiration date labels.

To prevent the wastage of food, we need to figure out a way to know when the food will be contaminated or spoiled. With the help of smart gas sensors that can sense gases and bacteria, the technological advancement of the present era has empowered us to identify food contamination and spoilage in advance.

The Technological advancement of IoT will deprecate expiry date because expiry dates are not reliable due to its dependency on multiple factors which includes but not limited to humidity, temperature, sunlight, storage conditions etc. Whereas IoT is bringing advanced technologies that can monitor food quality in real-time and provide predictive analysis of food's age too.

Food omit gases while it's getting contaminated/rotted and sensors sense the gases and identify whether the foods are spoiled or about to get spoiled which is impossible for human nose in most cases and it gets more difficult while Food Supply Chain. The following table provides a complete understanding of the Gas omission from the foods and sensors required to sense them:

Items	Gases	Sensors Required
Dairy products	NO2, H2S, CO, H2, CH4, CO, H2S	Hydrogen Sulfide H2S, CO, Nitrogen Dioxide NO2
Eggs	CO, Benzene, CH4, NH3, Gasoline, H2S, alcohol, H2	TGS-822, CO, MQ-8 Hydrogen Gas
Grains	H2, CH4, CO, H2S, Benzene	H2S, CO, H2 , MQ-4 Methane gas sensor
Olive oil	Hydrocarbons, methane, propane, chlorine	MQ-4 Methane gas sensor, Chlorine gas sensor.
Fruits and vegetables	NO2, Benzene H2, Propane, CH4, H2S, CO, H2S, CH4	Nitrogen dioxide sensor, H2S, CO
Meat	Methane, hydrogen sulfide, alcohol, carbon dioxide	MQ-4 Methane gas sensor, H2S, CO sensors

The five key realized business benefits in the food industry by utilizing IoT

1. Reduce food wastage by predictive analysis.
2. Maximize the shelf life of food by not depending on the expiry date.
3. Ensure bacterial protection by remotely monitoring and managing.
4. Retain good food quality by real-time monitoring during transportation and storage
5. Predict better food hygiene through historical analysis.

Sensor	Gas Detected	Business Usage	Price Range(USD)	Manufacturer/Provider	Website
TGS-822	Carbon Monoxide, Sulphur dioxide, alcohol, Ethanol, Gasoline, Methane,	Smoke and alcohol detectors	$7-10	JAPAN FIGARO	www.ebay.com
MH-Z14	CO2	Carbon dioxide detection	$79.99-85	Winsen	www.winsen-sensor.com
SHT10,11,15	Temperature, Humidity	Measure temperature and humidity	$1.89-4.74	Sensirion	www.sensirion.com
MQ131	Ozone	Air quality monitoring	$33.91	SPEC SENSORS	www.spec-sensors.com
C2H4 ethylene sensor	Ethylene	Used in ripening of fruits.	$378-385	Henan Inte Electrical Equipment Co., Ltd	www.intedetector.en.alibaba.com
NO sensor 4NO-250	Nitric Oxide	Food quality	$0.01-100	Shenzhen E-Best Industrial Co., Ltd.	www.e-best.en.alibaba.com
SO2	Sulfur Dioxide	To monitor pungent odorous gas.	$75-80	SPEC SENSORS	www.spec-sensors.com
CO	Carbon Monoxide	Air quality monitoring	$14.52	SPEC SENSORS	www.spec-sensors.com
MQ-8	Hydrogen Gas	To sense hydrogen concentrations in the air.	$7.95	Spark Fun	www.sparkfun.com

But the key question is how much these solutions are going to cost and most importantly are these sensors available or not. We have done some basic analysis and found following data on prices and providers of these sensors:

By leveraging IoT capabilities, we can create an effective food supply chain and will be able to control the climate (Temperature, humidity, bacteria, and gases) by analyzing containers and cargo trucks in real-time, that will reduce food spoilage and improve overall efficiency in the food supply-chain management.

7.5 IoT vs World Hunger

Feeding the growing world population is essential to the human race. The irony is that the production of food exceeds the demand by 20%, still,l we cannot feed our world population. What making things worse is the land that is available for agriculture/farming is shrinking and the demand for food is gradually increasing with the population increase.

Instead of just focusing on the production, we need to ensure that the food that is produced and available for consumption is not getting spoiled via effectively managing food supply chain and monitoring the food quality in real-time.

How IoT is making a huge dent to world hunger?

1. Agriculture under roof

The traditional outdoor agriculture is challenged by weather, drought, and disease whereas indoor farms can produce high output by using IoT technology for temperature control, humidifiers, pest control etc. IoT devices like moisture sensors and thermometers can provide real-time status of the farm environment and the crop.

2. Food Supply Chain/Logistic Management

As per UN's Food and Agriculture Organization (FAO), in developing countries, up to 30-40% of produced food usually gets wasted before even it reaches the market. Further, World Bank estimates that almost 90% of wasted calories from food are lost during storage and supply chain logistics. The IoT can make the distribution of food more effective by providing better monitoring and access to real-time data for decision-making.

3. Influencing food purchase habits

In IoT implemented world smart refrigerators will track food quantity and quality and can recommend purchase orders, even suggest the quality of food to be bought based on usage patterns. The Internet of Things (IoT) brings advantage in food production and logistics management with the introduction of IoT in Hospitality and IoT in the irrigation industry.

IoT helps in preventing the food from spoilage/contamination with the help of smart sensors connected to the cloud via gateways. The sensor data is analyzed to take preventive measures so that food doesn't get contaminated in the future.

Additional Interesting Reads about IoT

1. The most common confusion among business leaders is to pick which IoT Platform. But seeking the right IoT platform is not a right approach, Business leaders should opt for comprehensive IoT Solution.
2. The architecture plays a key role in IoT implementation. And we need to know what the architecture is, what it is consist of, and how it is going to work. to know about the IoT architecture.
3. The Transportation and Logistics industry is going through a big turmoil and IoT is helping the industry by making their business operation more effective and cost-efficient.
4. Efficient business operation and safety of the workforce and the environment are the major problems that the oil and gas industry is facing. With the implementation of Industrial IoT, the oil and gas industry is establishing a sustainable business model and providing a safer working environment for the workforce.

The Oil and Gas industry loses billions of USD yearly due to Non-Productive Time (NPT). IIoT solutions help companies reduce NPT events by using real-time data resulting in breakdown prediction and scheduling preventive maintenance. Industrial IoT is a revolutionary step in the evolution of the oil and gas industry. Data flows smoothly from grounds to boardrooms, enabling better decision making, better-optimized processes, and a safer working environment. In an industry that spends trillions of USD yearly on development, exploration, and asset maintenance, even a single-digit percentage improvement by implementation of IIoT will result in massive cost reduction.

If the right decision intelligence pipeline model of IoT is adopted then it can help leaders to make smarter business decisions. Hence, IIOT is not a just a buzzword and if implemented the right way, it could save thousands of lives.

7.6 IoT Trends that are Currently followed for Improved Agriculture

IoT technology is a disruptive technology providing immense growth in every industry. Smart farming is an emerging concept, which uses modern information and communication technologies to increase the product quantity and quality with easy optimization techniques.

Fig. 7.2: IoT Trends that are currently followed for Improved Agriculture

Sensor-based Farming

IoT is a smart technology that constitutes a combination of sensor devices, gateways, and communication protocols. Sensors are installed on fields to capture relevant data, which is stored on a cloud platform for further analysis. The farm managers have quick and easy access to the field data through their smart dashboards. Sensor-based farming provides improved strategies for farmers to effectively manage their farms.

Smart Livestock Management

With the advent of IoT technology, smart wearables for the animals are the new trend to keep a real-time check on their activities and health. Sensor-enabled techniques enable the farmers to keep a record of the animals' nutritional health, which prevents any kind of diseases or poor health. Using wireless IoT applications, farm owners can monitor the location of their cattle, and identify sick animals to prevent the spread of any disease.

Making Greenhouses Intelligent

Conventional means of creating greenhouses involve manual control of environmental parameters that might result in production losses, energy loss, or increased labor costs. Smart greenhouses are made up of IoT-driven techniques that can monitor every detail of crop production as well as climate control. It eliminates the need for manual processing due to its automated features and sensor-enabled capabilities. The sensors are installed to meet the specific requirements of the crops. These sensors capture data, which is processed through a cloud platform and can be controlled remotely.

Predicting Weather Conditions

Maintaining favorable weather conditions is an essential requirement for crop production. Combining various smart farming sensors with weather stations, it becomes easier to collect data from the environment and send it on the cloud platform. This data is used to map climatic conditions, and allow the farmers to take required measures and improve their production rate. IoT-enabled solutions use advanced algorithms to predict the weather conditions, allowing the farm management authorities to stay prepared according to the forecasts.

End-to-End Farm Management

With the use of IoT architecture and solutions, farm management has become easier and more advanced. From utilizing data-driven approaches to analyzing the information through a smart dashboard, IoT-based solutions provide end-to-end services to the farm authorities. There are several IoT-based applications for smart farm management like livestock tracking, warehouse monitoring, weather analysis, etc., which are designed to provide end-to-end farm services. Moreover, it is an effective way to improve farming activities to all extents.

Increased Investments

The farming sector is improving daily and its benefits are becoming more apparent, which directly attracts the number of investments in this sector. Many well-known original equipment manufacturers (OEMs) of sensor devices are introducing customized tracking tools and equipment to fulfill all the farm requirements. Also, several corporates are prepared to spend big on providing the agricultural industry with innovative technology, anticipating large ROI.

Smart Water Management

It is reported that 70% of the total freshwater supply is significantly used by the agricultural industry. This, in turn, creates the importance of optimizing water management with IoT technology. Installing technical solutions within the farming sector for smart irrigation helps cut down the wastage of water resources. Hence, improving the cost the fertilizer costs reduction at a significant level. The use of IoT technology provides adequate usage of water in the farms, which also helps in water conservation to a greater extent.

Usage of Drones

The rise and acceptance of IoT technology have promoted the concept of 'connected farms' at a significant level. The use of drones is gaining much importance as innovative tools to generate crop data and act as automatic supervising agents for cultivation lands. Most of the farming businesses are including drones to render better services and encourage smart farming. It is thus increasing the ability to make better and improved decisions for enhanced production.

Future of Farming: The Third Green Revolution

IoT technology is encouraging smart farming globally, which is significantly causing the third green revolution. The future of farming includes automated farm vehicles like tractors for better cultivation and improved sowing seeds under the ground. Also, with the use of GPS sensors in the vehicles, it becomes easier to locate their position and optimize the activities. With the rise in urbanization, using technology-driven solutions are designed to fulfill all the escalating food demands. IoT technology is potentially enabling better food traceability that will lead to increased food safety.

A few technological concepts like weeding robots, drones, automated harvesting, field analysis, and computerized imaging are extensively being used to improve agricultural practices and increase productivity. Since IoT technology uses sensors and gateways to extract information for improvement purposes; the farming sector is making the most out of it and increasing its productivity. Statistically, the **IoT applications in Agriculture** like precision farming, smart greenhouses, livestock monitoring, intelligent irrigation constitute an ever-growing market in the agriculture sector with a CAGR of 14.1% from 2019 till 2027. It is expected to reach approx. $34.9 billion by the end of 2027 and precision farming has accounted for the largest share of overall IoT applications in the agricultural market.

Purpose of Using IoT in Agriculture

The use of IoT in agriculture varies across the world in different aspects. The reason behind this difference lies in the acceptance of technological development in different parts of the world. Using IoT solutions in farming can provide you exponential growth and helps streamline your business. You can leverage large benefits by integrating advanced technologies like 5G, cloud computing with IoT solutions, and improve farming services.

The main idea behind enabling the Internet of Things for the farming sector is to inculcate automation and add a better scope for improved productivity. In terms of increased revenue, it is revealed that North America is the major contributor towards increasing digitization, technology awareness, and IoT acceptance by the farmers.

Using IoT technology can prove beneficial in all aspects of improving farming strategies and developing higher revenue. It works by utilizing the sensor devices and gateways for effective data extraction and communication throughout the processes. It is a system that consists of advanced sensors/devices, which connect through a cloud platform to process data into meaningful information. It further stores the data for convenient future access through connected gadgets and internet facilities.

The usage of IoT technology in the farming sector in mitigating the challenges like weather issues, farm management, pesticide requirements, crop quality, etc. It thereby provides a step forward to grow production in terms of best quality and revenue.

How a Smart Farming Solution Works and What are its Benefits?

A smart farming solution helps you manage all the possible farming activities through automation and smart techniques. You can install this solution to make intelligent decisions regarding crop yield quality, supply chain processes, warehouse monitoring, and livestock management. With IoT technology and its data-driven approach, you can even keep the farming equipment up to date and schedule prediction maintenance for better performance.

An **IoT-powered farming solution** works through high tech sensor devices. These devices get installed in appropriate places where data can be extracted. The data is then passed on a cloud platform through different kinds of communication channels and is processed into meaningful information. It is further displayed on the communicative dashboard of the user where they can perform analytics and gain actionable insights through push notifications or SMSs.

The solution is fully-fledged with the required sense of technology and provides immense benefits such as;

- Representative stats on livestock feeding and produce
- Geo-fencing and real-time tracking of the livestock
- Smart logistics and warehousing
- Remote crop monitoring
- Sensor-based field and resource mapping
- Smart greenhouses
- Intelligent pest management
- Weather forecasting
- Predictive analytics
- Remote equipment monitoring <

A smart farming solution resolves all your farm-related issues by improvising stock management, simplified data ingestion, smart contracts, and on-demand deliveries. It provides a personalized smartphone application for a user-friendly interaction across the entire farm. It also provides remote operability that helps save your time and offers cost-effective implementation of the solution.

Integrating a smart farming solution with your agricultural business enables intelligent tracking of the livestock. Moreover, the concept of geofencing is making it easier for farm managers to detect the presence of their livestock in any particular area. It is a smart technique that uses GPS tracking to locate the device present in any region.

The farming sector is increasing its worth by accepting IoT technology in multiple domains. It is redefining the existence of technology in managing farms, livestock, and producing quality crops. Being into the farm business, IoT-powered solutions allows better management strategies and maintaining the crop quality at every level. With the rising population and growing demands for food products, the IoT market size is expected to increase at significant levels for larger and quality produce.

Smart Fields: Better Management

The farming industry is eventually becoming more important with the advent of the Internet of Things technology. It is re-creating how farmers can plow, harvest, and maintain the crops. Moreover, the whole idea of transforming farms with technology is flourishing with smart IoT concepts. The farmers can track crop growth in real-time and keep a record for future analysis. This maintains the crop quality and suggests the requirements for healthy plant growth.

Precision Farming

Farmers, with the help of IoT, can employ high-tech farming techniques and smart solutions to improve the efficiency of their regular work. The Internet of Things uses sensor devices, which are installed in the fields for detailed supervision. These devices are smart, advanced, and allow the farmers to procure real-time information related to the topography and area resources. Moreover, the sensors also capture variable data such as acidity and soil temperature for better analysis.

Hence, IoT promotes precision farming and smart agriculture to predict the incoming weather conditions and assess the farm requirements to avoid any hindrance during farming activities. For instance, by installing an **IoT-powered farming solution**, the farmers can interconnect their smartphones and monitor their field activities remotely. It includes real-time monitoring of the farming equipment, crops, livestock, and visual representation through stats on the livestock feeding and produces. The solution also offers analytical and statistical insights for crops and livestock.

Smart Pest Management

Using traditional ways of manually inspecting the fields are long gone with the acceptance of IoT technology. In fields, pests damage the crops if left unidentified. Also, it becomes difficult for farm managers to supervise large fields regularly. Therefore, a smart IoT powered solution offers actionable insights to identify the pest areas and take necessary actions. Also, pesticides help prevent infestation but a small defect in the quality can also damage the crops. IoT, being an advanced technology, ensures that you use quality products to manage the crops and provides detailed analytics to identify swarm patterns.

Moreover, the Internet of Things is an advanced concept that provides alerts on crop health and growth quality. It ensures better control and maintenance of the crops to avoid spreading various diseases. The technology uses the abilities of sensor devices and smart dashboards to simplify the work for farmers and allow them to supervise the fields at their own pace. The installed sensor devices capture data from the fields and store it on a cloud platform for quick access. It enables smart functioning in the agricultural sector and makes way for improvements.

Intelligent Livestock Management

Farms include huge livestock and cattle, which require frequent supervision regarding their health and feeding habits. Smart wearables powered with IoT are widely used in the farms to keep a record of cattle health. Cows, horses, or other farm animals can wear smart neckbands, which are interconnected to an IoT dashboard and display health readings accurately. It allows the farmers to keep a real-time check on their blood pressure, temperature, and or any other health issues they might be facing.

Various animals are a part of farm management activities that require real-time monitoring of behavior that directly improves farm productivity. With the use of smart wearables and IoT solutions, you can track the feeding capacity and patterns, thereby making it easier for you to manage the livestock in better ways. Also, the quality production of milk and other proteins wholly depends on the health of the cattle. If you are feeding the cattle well, they are going to provide better results.

IoTized Farming – A Way Ahead

IoT is a futuristic technology, which is transforming the farming sector in multiple ways. Every asset that comprises a farm is increasing its potential with the usage of IoT solutions. Field management, crop monitoring, and livestock management have started accomplishing smarter and better with IoT. The Internet of Things reflects a brighter future for farming with a data-driven approach, maximized efficiency of equipment, and overall growth structure.

Moreover, the use of IoT technology also reduces waste output along with increased operational efficiency. Implementing smart solutions within the farming sector thus helps in exponentially increasing the quality products with better analytics, active insights, enhanced decision-making, and real-time data. You can also increase the potential of your fields by implementing IoT solutions and take the farming business to greater heights.

Pesticides and insecticides have played a major role in preventing infestations. However, they pose different environmental and social consequences. Extreme use of pesticides can result in severe water & soil contamination and can also intoxicate plants with harmful chemicals. Additionally, insects and bugs become reluctant against them with continuous exposure that forces farmers to rely on heavier pesticides. Even though other methods like genetic seed manipulation are also being used to make crops more robust against the pest attack, they are quite expensive for practical application.

Execution of Internet of Things in the agriculture sector has brought in a major development related to on-filed pest management. A farm owner can now use different sensors to monitor the growth of pests and take further countermeasures to manage them. Below is a list of different sensors that are being used to identify and track the growth of insects.

Sensor used for Pest Detection

1. Low-power Cameras and Sensors

Image capturing sensors for pest detection is famous among farmers due to its low cost and high return on investment. They install a low-cost image sensor in traps that captures the images of pests in it and send it to a centralized platform wirelessly. Based on the number of insects present in the traps, the farmers determine the location of insect infestation and take steps to remove them from fields. Along with its low cost, this sensor also offers advantages in terms of high scalability and mobility.

2. High-power Thermal Sensors

Low-power image sensors only click random images of insects that are visible from the naked eye. However, various pathogens ranging in millimeters also cause different crop diseases in the fields.

Thermography is a method that use thermal and infrared sensors to measure the amount of light reflected by a surface. Every surface reflects distinct amount of light energy which is also called its spectral signature. Plants and soil have a special spectral spectrum that is pre-recorded in spectrometers. In case a pathogen covers the surface of the plant leaves, the spectrum range of the plant will change indicating an attack by the pests. This method is highly effective in detecting the insects and their lifecycle stage. However, this method is expensive and sensitive to change in environmental conditions.

3. Fluorescence Image Sensing

In this method, the amount of chlorophyll present in a plant is measured based on its change in fluorescence parameters. An optical camera capture images of a plant leaves and then compare it with existing images of a healthy leaf. Change in chlorophyll patterns indicates the presence of pathogens or pests.

Even though, this method detects the presence of pests in a crop, its applicability in fields is highly limited due to scalability issues. Moreover, this method can only be used with crops that contain chlorophyll.

4. Acoustic Sensors

Detecting bugs and rodents through sound detection is another effective way to ensure plants quality. Wireless acoustic sensors situated at random locations in a field can pick up sound waves of insects. Locations with high sound waves indicate a higher concentration of bugs. A farmer can thus spray pesticides on these locations to ensure the quality of crops.

This cost-effective method offers high accuracy in detecting pest infestations and can be used at a wider scale. However, its accuracy depletes drastically in rainy and windy weather conditions.

5. Gas Sensors

Plants when stressed produce specific volatile chemical compounds. These compounds differ based on the stress that they feel. For instance, compound secreted due to environmental change will be different then the compound emanated due to pest infestation. Hence, these compounds have to be studied before they can be used for identifying attack caused due to bugs or rodents.

Once these compounds are studied, a gas sensor can be used to identify the attack by pests or type and nature of the infection. The only drawback with these methods is that of the sampling required to collect volatile compounds for data analysis.

7.7 Advantages Offered by IoT Based Pest Control Systems

These sensors are assisting farmers to target locations in their fields infected by insects and pathogens. The data collected through these sensors is instantly transferred to a centralized platform wirelessly. By using this platform, a farmer can monitor the health of its crop form distant locations and protect it from the attack of insects and rodents. The advantages offered by IoT to the agriculture sector in terms of pest control are:

1. Monitoring Pest Infestation and Crop Health

Through distant monitoring, a farmer can easily collect information about the presence of insects and rodents. Sensors placed in different corners of the field detect the infestation of pests or pathogens and transmit it to a dashboard. A farmer can use this dashboard to instantly connect with his fields and manage crop health.

Remote pest monitoring has drastically reduced manual inspection and random site visits. The farmers can now target areas that are affected by bugs and spray pesticides on required areas only. This considerably reduces the unnecessary use of pesticides, minimizing the chances of crop intoxication and environmental contamination. The collected data can also be used to identify the insects' breed and their population in the affected crop zones.

2. Weather monitoring and Analytics

The data gathered from pest detection sensors when recorded and analyzed properly can predict the attack by pests. Tracking the weather conditions and breeding patterns can also assist in identifying the threat level of pest populations.

During the breeding seasons, the probability of infestations is extreme. Moreover, rodents feed on crops to accumulate fat before they hibernate. Predictive analytics make use of such information to establish patterns and trends of probable pest outbreaks and swarm attacks. Based on the type of pest infestation and their population, the analytics feature can also recommend steps for future prevention and information for complete treatment.

3. Automated crop health monitoring

Integrated pest management (IPM) is a process that is encouraged to favor ecological, social, and economic consequences of pest control. It is an approach that focuses on the limited usage of pesticides to manage pest damage and incur the least possible pesticide-related hazards.

The implementation of IoT in the IPM system will automate time-consuming operations such as manual data point measurement and inspection. Automation makes the process more accurate, cost-effective, and assist farmers to take instant actions based on the response from the sensors. Use of pesticides will also be optimized which will further decrease environmental contamination and harm to crop health.

It is important for a farm owner to control and remove pests from its field to ensure crop health. The advent of IoT in the agriculture sector has enabled a farmer to remotely monitor and control pest infestation. With a one-time investment, a farmer can integrate an IoT powered pest control system to its farm and accurately detect the presence of bugs and rodents without manual inspection. However, the complete capability of IoT in farming rests with the combined usage of its agriculture-based applications. Distant pest control along with crop management, weather monitoring, and livestock management is enabling the development of various modern farming approaches that were never witnessed by the agriculture sector in the past.

Agriculturists and farmers know the importance of maintaining optimum nutrition and moisture level of the soil to facilitate the growth of crops. Use of fertilizers and manures improves soil's quality and a robust irrigation system facilitates controlling the water content in it. Advancements in Internet of Things and sensor technology has given rise to various soil moisture detection systems. By using these devices a farmer can monitor and manage the quality of his soil and choose a crop that is suitable to grow on his fields. There are different mechanisms that these sensors used to determine soil water content. It is therefore important to be familiar with different terminologies related to soil moisture.

Recent statistics reveal that the global population is about to reach 9.6 billion by 2050. And to feed this massive population, the agriculture industry is bounded to adopt the Internet of Things. Amongst the challenges like extreme weather conditions, climatic changes, environmental impact, IoT is eradicating these challenges and helping us to meet the demand for more food.

Throughout the world, mechanical innovations such as tractors and harvesters took place and brought into the agriculture operations in the late 20th century. And the agriculture Industry relies heavily on innovative ideas because of the steadily growing demand for food.

The Industrial IoT has been a driving force behind increased agricultural production at a lower cost. In the next several years, the use of smart solutions powered by IoT will increase in the agriculture operations. In fact, few of the recent report tells that the IoT device installation will see a compound annual growth rate of 20% in the agriculture industry. And the no. of connected devices (agricultural) will grow from 13 million in 2014 to 225 million by 2024.

Due to lack of constant and reliable communication network infrastructure, an **IoT solutions provider** as well as the business owners had faced implementation challenges in remote or less developed regions. But, many network providers are making it possible by introducing satellite connectivity

Data can be obtained by corresponding sensors and detectors and then transferred to the main server for processing. In physical implementation the major components are the sensors and network for accurate data transmission. Growers setup the different monitoring devices and sensors according to the specific requirements and track or record the required information. Agriculturists make better decisions by analyzing the received information and achieve specific goals by obtaining optimal data. There are many IoT based greenhouse applications such as

In today's modern world everything needs to be automatic with less man power by consuming less time. Sensor is such a device which can fulfill this requirement by detecting same input from the existing physical environment and responds back. User set some setting over sensing devices to perform their task without the involvement of human. There are some major IoT sensors like: Motion Detector, PIR, Soil Moisture, Temperature, Humidity, Barometric Pressure, Ultra Violet, PH, and gas sensor. In Table 3 various sensor based agricultural applications, their operations and IoT association have been discussed but table 2 pay attention only on smart phone agricultural apps.

References

A. Hemmat, A.R. Binandeh, J. Ghaisari, and A. Khorsandi, "Development and field testing of an integrated sensor for on-the-go measurement of soil mechanical resistance," Sensors and Actuators A: Physical, vol. 198, pp. 61–68, 2013.

A. Hoglund, X. Lin, O. Liberg et al., "Overview of 3GPP release 14 enhanced NB-IoT," IEEE Network, vol. 31, no. 6, pp. 16–22, 2017.

A. Kamilaris and F. X. Prenafeta-Boldú, "Deep learning in agriculture: a survey," Computers and Electronics in Agriculture, vol. 147, pp. 70–90, 2018.

A. M. Jawad, H. M. Jawad, R. Nordin, S. K. Gharghan, N. F. Abdullah, and M. J. Abu-Alshaeer, "Wireless power transfer with magnetic resonator coupling and sleep/active strategy for a drone charging station in smart agriculture," Access, vol. 7, pp. 139839–139851, 2019.

B. Dai, Y. He, F. Gu, L. Yang, J. Han, and W. Xu, "A vision-based autonomous aerial spray system for precision agriculture," in 2017 IEEE International Conference on Robotics and Biomimetics, ROBIO, pp. 1–7, Macau, Macao, 2017.

B. H. Y. Alsalam, K. Morton, D. Campbell, and F. Gonzalez, "Autonomous UAV with vision based on-board decision making for remote sensing and precision agriculture," in 2017 IEEE Aerospace Conference, pp. 1–12, Big Sky, MT, USA, 2017.

B. Keswani, A.G. Mohapatra, A. Mohanty et al., "Adapting weather conditions based IoT enabled smart irrigation technique in precision agriculture mechanisms," Neural Computing and Applications, vol. 31, no. S1, pp. 277–292, 2019.

B. L. Risteska Stojkoska and K. V. Trivodaliev, "A review of Internet of things for smart home: challenges and solutions," Journal of Cleaner Production, vol. 140, pp. 1454–1464, 2017.

B. S. Faiçal, H. Freitas, P. H. Gomes et al., "An adaptive approach for UAV-based pesticide spraying in dynamic environments," Computers and Electronics in Agriculture, vol. 138, pp. 210–223, 2017.

B. Vejlgaard, M. Lauridsen, H. Nguyen, I. Z. Kovács, P. Mogensen, and M. Sorensen, "Coverage and capacity analysis of sigfox, lora, gprs, and nb-iot," in 2017 IEEE 85th vehicular technology conference (VTC Spring), pp. 1–5, Sydney, NSW, Australia, 2017.

B. Y. Suprapto, M. A. Heryanto, H. Suprijono, J. Muliadi, and B. Kusumoputro, "Design and development of heavy-lift hexcopter for heavy payload," in 2017 International Seminar on Application for Technology of Information and Communication (iSemantic), pp. 242–246, Semarang Indonesia, 2017.

D. J. Cocovi-Solberg, M. Rosende, and M. Miró, "Automatic kinetic bioaccessibility assay of lead in soil environments using flow-through microdialysis as a front end to electrothermal atomic absorption spectrometry," Environmental Science & Technology, vol. 48, no. 11, pp. 6282–6290, 2014.

D. Sinwar, V.S. Dhaka, M.K. Sharma, and G. Rani, AI-based yield prediction and smart irrigation, Springer, Singapore, 2020.

D. W. Sambo, A. Forster, B.O. Yenke, I. Sarr, B. Gueye, and P. Dayang, "Wireless underground sensor networks path loss model for precision agriculture (WUSN-PLM)," IEEE Sensors Journal, vol. 20, no. 10, pp. 5298–5313, 2020.

E. Husni, G.B. Hertantyo, D.W. Wicaksono, F.C. Hasibuan, A.U. Rahayu, and M.A. Triawan, "Applied Internet of things (IoT): car monitoring system using IBM BlueMix," in 2016 International Seminar on Intelligent Technology and Its Applications (ISITIA), pp. 417–422, Lombok, Indonesia, 2017.

E. Suganya, S. Sountharrajan, S. K. Shandilya, and M. Karthiga, "IoT in agriculture investigation on plant diseases and nutrient level using image analysis techniques," Internet of Things in Biomedical Engineering, Academic Press, pp. 117–130, 2019.

Earth has lost a third of arable land in past 40 years, scientists say|Environment|The Guardian, https://www.theguardian.com/environment/2015/dec/02/arable-land-soil-food-security-shortage.

F. Adelantado, X. Vilajosana, P. Tuset-Peiro, B. Martinez, J. Melia-Segui, and T. Watteyne, "Understanding the limits of LoRaWAN," IEEE Communications Magazine, vol. 55, no. 9, pp. 34–40, 2017.

F. Castaldi, F. Pelosi, S. Pascucci, and R. Casa, "Assessing the potential of images from unmanned aerial vehicles (UAV) to support herbicide patch spraying in maize," Precision Agriculture, vol. 18, no. 1, pp. 76–94, 2017.

F. Ghavimi and H.-H. Chen, "M2M communications in 3GPP LTE/LTE-A networks: architectures, service requirements, challenges, and applications," IEEE Communications Surveys & Tutorials, vol. 17, no. 2, pp. 525–549, 2014.

F. Vanegas, D. Bratanov, K. Powell, J. Weiss, and F. Gonzalez, "A novel methodology for improving plant pest surveillance in vineyards and crops using UAV-based hyperspectral and spatial data," Sensors, vol. 18, no. 1, p. 260, 2018.

Fixed-wing drone, UAV for long-range commercial applications|Applied Aeronautics, April 2020, https://www.unmannedsystemstechnology.com/company/applied-aeronautics/.

G. Sierra, M. Orchard, K. Goebel, and C. Kulkarni, "Battery health management for small-size rotary-wing electric unmanned aerial vehicles: an efficient approach for constrained computing platforms," Reliability Engineering and System Safety, vol. 182, pp. 166–178, 2019.

G. Sona, D. Passoni, L. Pinto et al., "UAV multispectral survey to map soil and crop for precision farming applications," https://air.unimi.it/handle/2434/451326.

Growing at a slower pace, world population is expected to reach 9.7 billion in 2050 and could peak at nearly 11 billion around 2100|UN DESA|United Nations Department of Economic and Social Affairs, April 2020, https://www.un.org/development/desa/en/news/population/world-population-prospects-2019.html.

H. Arasteh, V. Hosseinnezhad, V. Loia et al., "Iot-based smart cities: a survey," in 2016 IEEE 16th international conference on environment and electrical engineering (EEEIC), pp. 1–6, Italy, 2016.

H. Huang, J. Deng, Y. Lan, A. Yang, X. Deng, and L. Zhang, "A fully convolutional network for weed mapping of unmanned aerial vehicle (UAV) imagery," PLoS One, vol. 13, no. 4, article e0196302, 2018.

H. M. Jawad, A. M. Jawad, R. Nordin et al., "Accurate empirical path-loss model based on particle swarm optimization for wireless sensor networks in smart agriculture," IEEE Sensors Journal, vol. 20, no. 1, pp. 552–561, 2020.

H. Obasekore, M. Fanni, and S. M. Ahmed, "Insect killing robot for agricultural purposes," IEEE/ASME International Conference on Advanced Intelligent Mechatronics, AIM, vol. 2019, pp. 1068–1074, 2019.

H. S. Mahmood, M. Ahmad, T. Ahmad, M. A. Saeed, and M. Iqbal, "Potentials and prospects of precision agriculture in Pakistan-a review," Pakistan Journal of Agricultural Research, vol. 26, no. 2, pp. 151–167, 2013.

H. Sharma, M.K. Shukla, R. Steiner, M.K. Shukla, and P. W. Bosland, "Soil moisture sensor calibration, actual evapotranspiration, and crop coefficients for drip irrigated greenhouse chile peppers," Agricultural Water Management, vol. 179, pp. 81–91, 2017.

How to grow four tons of food a year in a metal box without sunlight|MIT Technology Review, May 2020, https://www.technologyreview.com/2018/03/08/3213/how-to-grow-four-tons-of-food-a-year-in-a-metal-box-without-sunlight/#Echobox=1582745134.

Inside London's first underground farm|The Independent, May 2020, https://www.independent.co.uk/Business/indyventure/growing-underground-london-farm-food-waste-first-food-miles-a7562151.html.

J. A. Manrique, J. S. Rueda-Rueda, and J. M. T. Portocarrero, "Contrasting Internet of things and wireless sensor network from a conceptual overview," in 2016 IEEE international conference on Internet of Things (iThings) and IEEE green computing and communications (GreenCom) and IEEE cyber, physical and social computing (CPSCom) and IEEE smart data (SmartData), pp. 252–257, Chengdu, China, 2017.

J. Navia, I. Mondragon, D. Patino, and J. Colorado, "Multispectral mapping in agriculture: terrain mosaic using an autonomous quadcopter UAV," in 2016 International Conference on Unmanned Aircraft Systems, ICUAS 2016, pp. 1351–1358, Arlington, VA, USA, 2016.

J. Senthilnath, M. Kandukuri, A. Dokania, and K. N. Ramesh, "Application of UAV imaging platform for vegetation analysis based on spectral-spatial methods," Computers and Electronics in Agriculture, vol. 140, pp. 8–24, 2017.

J. Torres-Sánchez, J. M. Peña, A. I. de Castro, and F. López-Granados, "Multi-temporal mapping of the vegetation fraction in early-season wheat fields using images from UAV," Computers and Electronics in Agriculture, vol. 103, pp. 104–113, 2014.

K. Ivushkin, H. Bartholomeus, A. K. Bregt et al., "UAV based soil salinity assessment of cropland," Geoderma, vol. 338, pp. 502–512, 2019.

Key facts-world urbanization prospects-population division-United Nations April 2020, https://population.un.org/wup/Publications/Files/WUP2018-Key Facts.pdf.

Khattab, S. E. D. Habib, H. Ismail, S. Zayan, Y. Fahmy, and M. M. Khairy, "An IoT-based cognitive monitoring system for early plant disease forecast," Computers and Electronics in Agriculture, vol. 166, article 105028, 2019.

M. A. Hassan, M. Yang, A. Rasheed et al., "A rapid monitoring of NDVI across the wheat growth cycle for grain yield prediction using a multi-spectral UAV platform," Plant Science, vol. 282, pp. 95–103, 2019.

M. Lu, M. Bagheri, A. P. James, and T. Phung, "Wireless charging techniques for UAVs: a review, reconceptualization, and extension," IEEE Access, vol. 6, pp. 29865–29884, 2018.

M. N. Boukoberine, Z. Zhou, and M. Benbouzid, "A critical review on unmanned aerial vehicles power supply and energy management: solutions, strategies, and prospects," Applied Energy, vol. 255, article 113823, 2019.

M. N. Muhammad, A. Wayayok, A. R. Mohamed Shariff, A. F. Abdullah, and E. M. Husin, "Droplet deposition density of organic liquid fertilizer at low altitude UAV aerial spraying in rice cultivation," Computers and Electronics in Agriculture, vol. 167, article 105045, 2019.

M. P. Wachowiak, D. F. Walters, J. M. Kovacs, R. Wachowiak-Smolíková, and A. L. James, "Visual analytics and remote sensing imagery to support community-based research for precision agriculture in emerging areas," Computers and Electronics in Agriculture, vol. 143, pp. 149–164, 2017.

M. R. Yousefi, "Application of GIS and GPS in precision agriculture (a review)," May 2020, http://www.ijabbr.com/.

M. S. Mekala, V. Perumal, M. Shareef Mekala, and P. Viswanathan, "A survey: smart agriculture IoT with cloud computing," in 2017 international conference on microelectronic devices, circuits and systems (ICMDCS), pp. 1–7, Vellore, India, 2017.

Making every drop count: Pakistan's growing water scarcity challenge|IISD, May 2020, https://www.iisd.org/library/making-every-drop-count-pakistan-s-growing-water-scarcity-challenge.

Ministry of Finance|Government of Pakistan|Pakistan Economic Survey 2018-19-Agriculture, May 2020, http://finance.gov.pk/survey_1819.html.

N. Baker, "ZigBee and Bluetooth: strengths and weaknesses for industrial applications," Computing & Control Engineering Journal, vol. 16, no. 2, pp. 20–25, 2005.

O. A. Denton, V. O. Aduramigba-Modupe, A. O. Ojo et al., "Assessment of spatial variability and mapping of soil properties for sustainable agricultural production using geographic information system techniques (GIS)," Cogent Food & Agriculture, vol. 3, no. 1, 2017.

Paris is opening the world's largest urban rooftop farm|World Economic Forum, May 2020, https://www.weforum.org/agenda/2019/08/vertical-urban-farm-city-paris.

Q. F. Hassan, Internet of things A to Z: technologies and applications-concepts and perspectives, Wiley-IEEE Press, 2018.

Restorative farm produces food, fresh water, and clean energy in the desert - Science, May 2020, https://pk.mashable.com/science/1003/restorative-farm-produces-food-fresh-water-and-clean-energy-in-the-desert.

S. A. Imam, A. Choudhary, and V. K. Sachan, "Design issues for wireless sensor networks and smart humidity sensors for precision agriculture: a review," International Conference on Soft Computing Techniques and Implementations, ICSCTI, vol. 2016, pp. 181–187, 2015.

S. Aldhaher, P. D. Mitcheson, J. M. Arteaga, G. Kkelis, and D. C. Yates, "Light-weight wireless power transfer for mid-air charging of drones," in 2017 11th European Conference on Antennas and Propagation (EUCAP), pp. 336–340, Paris, France, 2017.

S. Athani, C. H. Tejeshwar, M. M. Patil, P. Patil, and R. Kulkarni, "Soil moisture monitoring using IoT enabled Arduino sensors with neural networks for improving soil management for farmers and predict seasonal rainfall for planning future harvest in North Karnataka-India," Proceedings of the International Conference on IoT in Social, Mobile, Analytics and Cloud, I-SMAC, vol. 2017, pp. 43–48, 2017.

S. B. Baker, W. Xiang, and I. Atkinson, "Internet of things for smart healthcare: technologies, challenges, and opportunities," IEEE Access, vol. 5, pp. 26521–26544, 2017.

S. C. Murray, "Optical sensors advancing precision in agricultural production," Photonics Spectra, vol. 51, no. 6, pp. 48–56, 2017.

S. Diwate, V. Nitnaware, and K. Argulwar, "Design and development of application specific drone machine for seed sowing," International Research Journal of Engineering and Technology, vol. 5, no. 5, pp. 4003–4007, 2018.

S. Park, D. Ryu, S. Fuentes, H. Chung, E. Hernández-Montes, and M. O'Connell, "Adaptive estimation of crop water stress in nectarine and peach orchards using high-resolution imagery from an unmanned aerial vehicle (UAV)," Remote Sensing, vol. 9, no. 8, p. 828, 2017.

S. R. Pokhrel and C. Williamson, "Modeling compound TCP over WiFi for IoT," IEEE/ACM Transactions on Networking, vol. 26, no. 2, pp. 864–878, 2018.

S. Verma, A. Bhatia, A. Chug, and A. P. Singh, "Recent advancements in multimedia big data computing for IoT applications in precision agriculture: opportunities, issues, and challenges," Multimedia Big Data Computing for IoT Applications, Springer, Singapore, pp. 391–416, 2020.

Sixty Eight percent of the world population projected to live in urban areas by 2050, says UN|UN DESA|United Nations Department of Economic and Social Affairs, April 2020, https://www.un.org/development/desa/en/news/population/2018-revision-of-world-urbanization-prospects.html.

T. M. Mostafa, A. Muharam, and R. Hattori, "Wireless battery charging system for drones via capacitive power transfer," in 2017 IEEE PELS Workshop on Emerging Technologies: Wireless Power Transfer (WoW), pp. 1–6, Chongqing, China, 2017.

Tasmanian farmers use drones to make irrigation more efficient - ABC News, May 2020, https://www.abc.net.au/news/2017-07-27/drone-technology-on-farms/8746272.

The Netherlands is a leader in sustainable agriculture|World Economic Forum, May 2020, https://www.weforum.org/agenda/2019/11/netherlands-dutch-farming-agriculture-sustainable.

The Path to 5G with LTE-M and NB-IoT|Sierra Wireless," May 2020, https://www.sierrawireless.com/iot-blog/iot-blog/2018/05/lte-m-nb-iot-5g-networks/.

W. H. Maes and K. Steppe, "Perspectives for remote sensing with unmanned aerial vehicles in precision agriculture," Trends in Plant Science, vol. 24, no. 2, pp. 152–164, 2019.

www.academia.edu/.../GLOBALISATION_AND_ITS_POSITIVE_IMPACT

www.epw.in/discussion/globalisation-indian-agriculture.html

X. Feng, F. Yan, and X. Liu, "Study of wireless communication technologies on Internet of things for precision agriculture," Wireless Personal Communications, vol. 108, no. 3, pp. 1785–1802, 2019.

Yield losses due to pests, May 2020, https://blog.agrivi.com/post/yield-losses-due-to-pests.